Believers are often disappointed with their Christian walk. They long for a solution to repeated failures in their day-to-day experiences, but somehow the solution seems to elude them.

There is a solution and it can be found in a study of the Epistle of James. Travel with the author through this book and discover how you can experience victory and not defeat as you demonstrate your faith in every day actions.

Let the study of James change your life. You will then begin *walking what you're talking*.

WALKING WHAT YOU'RE TALKING

Principles from James

A Regal Bible Commentary for Laymen

HAROLD L. FICKETT

Regal Books

A Division of GL Publications
Ventura, California, U.S.A.

Published by Regal Books
A Division of GL Publications
Ventura, California 93006
Printed in U.S.A.

Originally published under the title *James: Faith that Works.*

Library of Congress Cataloging-in-Publication data.

Fickett, Harold L.
    Walking what you're talking (principles of James)

    Bibliography: p.
    1. Bible. N.T. James—Commentaries. I. Title.
BS2785.3.F52   1988   227'.91077   88-18544
ISBN 0-8307-1298-4

Any omission of credits or permissions is unintentional. The publisher and
author request documentation for future printings.

CONTENTS

INTRODUCTION

What is James? The book of James is one of the strongest pleas for vital Christianity in the New Testament. Bible scholars are generally agreed that the Epistle of James with the possible exception of Mark was the first new Testament book written. The date of its writing falls somewhere between A.D. 45 and 50, approximately 15 to 20 years after the ascension of Jesus.

And just who is James? Who is this individual whom the Spirit of God used to write this practical and important book? There are five men in the New Testament who are called by this name: James, the father of the apostle Judas; James, the son of Zebedee; James, the son of Cleophas; James, the Less; and James, the brother of the Lord and the son of Mary and Joseph.

It is generally agreed that James, the brother of the Lord, is the man referred to in James 1:1. However, there are three different theories to explain the meaning of the word *brother*.

First, the Hieronymian theory says that when the Bible speaks of James as a brother of Jesus, it really means cousin. This would make James, the son of Cleophas, the author of this book. This can not be correct because the word used for brother is *adelphos*, which always refers to a blood brother. Instead of making James the son of Cleophas and James the brother of Jesus the same person, *adelphos* clearly distinguishes between them.

Second, the Epiphanian theory, suggested in A.D.

370, is based on a legend of an elderly couple who had no children. In their old age God blessed them with a girl, Mary, who became the virgin mother of Christ. When Mary was 12 the High Priest at the Temple arranged her marriage to an elderly widower, Joseph. He loved Mary in the sense of protecting her and providing for her. His children by his first marriage became the half brothers and sisters of Jesus. One of these was James. The accounts of the birth of Christ in Matthew and Luke refute this legend. Matthew 1:25 tells us Joseph did not know Mary until *after* the birth of Jesus. Jesus is called a firstborn son, which indicates other children. Matthew 13:53-58 and Mark 6:1-6 tell us James was one of these.

Third, the Helvidius theory simply states that after the virgin birth of Christ, Joseph and Mary lived together as man and wife. They had other sons and daughters, one of whom was James, the author of the Epistle of James.

The first two theories, the Hieronymian and the Epiphanian, were developed to protect the false doctrine that Mary was perpetually a virgin. Scripture teaches that after the miraculous birth of Jesus, Mary and Joseph became the parents of other sons and daughters by natural procreation. One of these was James who is the author of this book.

CHAPTER ONE

TURNING A NEGATIVE INTO A POSITIVE

JAMES 1:1-4,12

JAMES 1:1-4,12

1. James, a bond-servant of God and of the Lord Jesus Christ, to the twelve tribes who are dispersed abroad, greetings.
2. Consider it all joy, my brethren, when you encounter various trials;
3. knowing that the testing of your faith produces endurance.
4. And let endurance have *its* perfect result, that you may be perfect and complete, lacking in nothing.
12. Blessed is a man who perseveres under trial; for once he has been approved, he will receive the crown of life, which *the Lord* has promised to those who love him.

The most practical approach to Christian living in the Bible appears in the book of James. It was written for the benefit of believers and spells out specifically what God expects of Christians. In the 108 verses of this book, there are 60 commands from Almighty God for Christians.

VERSE 1

In the first verse of James there are three basic Christian concepts: Christian conversion, Christian service and Christian worldwide fellowship.

Conversion

Prior to the crucifixion of Jesus, James and his other brothers and sisters were not converted. In spite of the miracles Jesus performed and the circumspect life He lived, His immediate family refused to acknowledge Him to be whom He claimed to be, the Son of God and the Savior of the world.

However, James eventually changed. He suggests the concept of conversion in the Epistle's first word. James is no longer a skeptic. He is confirmed in the faith and is a leader in the Christian movement.

Service

Christian service is suggested by the description James gives himself. James is the only New Testament writer who refers to himself as a servant without listing any other qualifications. After his conversion James considered himself to be nothing more than a servant of God and of the Lord Jesus Christ.

The word *bond-servant* in this verse comes from the Greek word *doulos* signifying absolute obedience, total surrender and complete loyalty. Most people rebel at this thought. They are willing to be partially obedient, but not completely so.

A British lady said, "I want the Lord to be my Constitutional King, but I want to be the Prime Minister." She was aware that the Constitutional King is only a figurehead, while it is the Prime Minister who governs. Many Christians want the Lord to be only a figurehead. They want Him there to bless them and to meet their needs while at the same time they continue governing themselves.

Doulos also is used to indicate one who is in the line

of succession, such as the prophets of old. It is one of the titles ascribed to the greats of the Old Testament. In this context then, complete loyalty comes from those people who are faithful even unto death in implementing the will of the Lord. Just think of it! When a person truly surrenders to God and the Lord Jesus, he stands shoulder to shoulder in history with men like Abraham, Moses, Jacob, Samuel, Elijah, Elisha, Isaiah and Jeremiah.

Fellowship

The worldwide fellowship of Christians first began many hundreds of years ago when God scattered His chosen people throughout the known world. In 722 B.C. the Assyrians captured the 10 northern tribes of Israel and deported many of them to Assyria. During the time of Nebuchadnezzar, there was a voluntary exodus of many Jews to Egypt. This began in 650 B.C. and continued for a number of years.

The next general scattering of God's people took place between 605 and 587 B.C. During these years the Babylonians under the leadership of Nebuchadnezzar conquered Judah with its capital at Jerusalem. From the time of the Assyrian captivity until the birth of Christ, there was a small but steady voluntary migration of Jews to Syria. In addition to all of this, in 67 B.C. Pompey conquered Jerusalem and deported many Palestinians to the city of Rome.

These Jewish people moving out of Palestine and into new communities maintained their identity. They continued to practice Judaism, the foundation of Christianity, and were never absorbed by the foreign populations.

When Christ came announcing that He was the fulfill-ment of the Old Testament prophecies regarding the coming of the Messiah, there were people in nearly every community of the then known world who were at least familiar enough with the teaching of the Old Testa-ment to give honest consideration to this announce-ment. In other words, God had prepared a ready-made worldwide mission field where the gospel could effec-tively be preached.

Not by any stretch of the imagination did all of the Jews of the world accept Jesus as the Messiah. Out of their synagogues, however, came the first converts to Christianity. It wasn't long after the inception of the Chris-tian movement that there was a worldwide fellowship of believers made up of converts from Judaism. It was to these people that James addressed his Epistle.

VERSE 2

The first problem James discusses is that of the Chris-tian facing temptation. There are two meanings of the word. *Temptation (KJV)* means a testing for the purpose of strengthening and purifying and proving faith. A young bird tests its wings when it flies off the nest. When the Queen of Sheba visited Solomon, she came to put his wisdom to a test with hard questions (see 1 Kings 10:1). Abraham's faith was tested when he was directed to sacrifice his son, Isaac (see Gen. 22:1,2).

Temptation also means solicitation to do wrong, the enticement of an individual to commit sin and the encouragement of a person to do that which is contrary to the will of God for his life.

James deals with both types of temptation. In verses 2-4 and 12 he discusses the Christian facing temptation in the sense of a testing and a proving experience. In verses 13-15 he gives attention to the Christian facing temptation in the sense of an allurement to commit sin.

Testing

In verse 2 James talks about what the Christian's attitude should be toward a testing experience. There are two words in this verse to notice especially: *consider* and *various*. By using the word *various*, James is saying what Christians all know through experience to be true. He is saying that without exception all of us in the course of our lives will be confronted with numerous and various types of testing. These tests will come in the form of ill health, of disappointed friendships, of sorrow due to the loss of loved ones, of financial reverses and of failure on the part of family members not to live up to our expectations.

James makes the amazing assertion that Christians are to "*consider* it all joy" when faced with these various temptations. Common sense dictates that he is not telling them to rejoice in the face of the testing experience. No one in his right mind rejoices because the doctor tells him he has cancer. No one can possibly be happy when a friend betrays him. It is impossible for an individual to be jubilant over the death of a loved one. Financial reverses are never a source of abounding ecstasy. No one can be hilarious over a member of his family bringing ill repute to the family name.

So what is James trying to say when he points out that Christians are to consider it all joy when various testings come their way? Dr. Spiros Zodhiates answers this question, "The word (consider) should rather be translated, 'think forward, consider, regard.' As you live in the present consider the future, think forward to the future. Gloom now, but glory in the days to come."[1]

Both in the crucifixion of Christ and in His teaching, Christians have a perfect explanation of joy in testing. The excruciating pain of the cross was not a source of rejoicing to the Master. He was joyful in the experience because of His ability to look forward to the future and realize what His crucifixion would accomplish.

In the Beatitudes from the Sermon on the Mount the Master did not tell His disciples that they were to rejoice in the persecution itself. Instead, He asked them to find their blessing or happiness in the reward that would be theirs in the future (see Matt. 5:1-11).

VERSE 3

James goes on to say what the correct attitude on the part of a Christian facing temptation will produce in his life. Simply stated it is the virtue of patience. A young minister, realizing his lack of patience, once asked a more experienced preacher to pray with him about this problem. The aged man of God knelt with the young man and began to ask the Lord to send troubles and difficulties into his young friend's life. As he continued along this line, the younger minister tapped him on the shoulder and whispered, "You must have misunderstood me. I asked that you would pray that I might have more patience, not more trouble." The experienced minister responded, "The Scriptures say, 'Tribulation worketh patience,' that is the only way." (Rom. 5:3 KJV).

A careful study of patience reveals an active and a passive connotation. Passive patience pictures the person who is under pressure refusing to flee. He remains, he stands fast and he accepts what comes to him.

The Christian who allows patience to do its perfect work in him will live constantly on the victory side of life.

Through it all he has about him an air of contentment and satisfaction.

Commenting on the active nature of patience, William Barclay wrote, "It is not simply the ability to bear things; it is the ability to turn them to greatness and glory. The thing which amazed the heathen in the centuries of persecution was that the martyrs did not die grimly, they died singing."[2]

Back in 1941 a Japanese man by the name of Manken Ishii retired from the restaurant business in New York City. He felt God wanted him to beautify Ulster County where he lived by raising cherry trees and giving them to his friends and neighbors. This he did until 1956 when he had a severe fall and fractured his spine. For seven days and nights he lay paralyzed in a hospital bed unable to eat, drink or talk to visitors.

Manken recalls, "There was only one thing I could do and that was pray. This I did every minute. The pain became so intense that I actually asked the Lord to take me home. Then when I thought I had died and gone to heaven, God revealed to me that such was not the case. He wanted me to recover and make my land a flowering country. From then on I began to fight against this malady. Finally I was victorious over it. I set as my goal the raising and giving away of 100,000 cherry trees in 10 years. In just a little more than six years I accomplished my goal. Now my goal is 1,000,000. I shall continue to serve my Lord in this way as long as He gives me breath."

VERSES 4, 12

In verses 4 and 12, James spells out the results that will accrue in the life of the Christian who possesses the virtue of patience. James says this person will be perfect. Obviously this does not mean he will be sinless. Rather it means he will be mature. The Christian in whose life patience has worked becomes mature in Christ Jesus.

Fit for Service

The Christian will be *complete*. This has to do with the fitness of a person for Christian service. In the Bible it is used to describe a priest who is qualified to offer sacrifices unto God. He is one who has met God's standards and fulfilled the requirements of this office.

The Christian possessing patience will lack nothing. James says that the Christian who allows patience to do its perfect work in him will not be defeated. He will live constantly on the victory side of life. He won't be bitter, disgruntled and pessimistic. Instead he will be vivacious, energetic and buoyant. He will be eager to get on with the job that God has given him to do, for he has assurance that he will receive a crown of life which the Lord has promised to them that love Him.

Crown of Life

In the ancient world, the crown signified at least four things: joy, royalty, victory and honor. These four concepts tell the story of the patient Christian's eternal reward. Because of his faith in Christ, he will win the victory over sin and death. He will be ushered into the presence of the Lord where as royalty he will share in the eternal inheritance of the King of kings. He will be elevated to a place of honor. All of this will result in his experiencing unspeakable, indescribable, everlasting joy.

FOR REFLECTION

What are the three basic Christian concepts in the first verse of James?

Describe the attitude a Christian should have when facing temptation.

Footnotes
1. Spiros Zodhiates, *The Work of Faith* (Grand Rapids: Wm. B. Eerdmans Publishing Co.). Used by permission.
2. *The Letters of James and Peter,* translated and interpreted by William Barclay. Published by the Saint Andrew Press, Edinburgh, 1958; and in the U.S.A. by the Westminster Press, 1961, p. 51.

CHAPTER TWO

TAPPING THE SOURCE

JAMES 1:5-11

5. But if any of you lacks wisdom, let him ask of God, who gives to all men generously and without reproach, and it will be given to him.
6. But let him ask in faith without any doubting, for the one who doubts is like the surf of the sea driven and tossed by the wind.
7. For let not that man expect that he will receive anything from the Lord,
8. *being* a double-minded man, unstable in all his ways.
9. But let the brother of humble circumstances glory in his high position;
10. and *let* the rich man *glory* in his humiliation, because like flowering grass he will pass away.
11. For the sun rises with a scorching wind, and withers the grass; and its flower falls off, and the beauty of its appearance is destroyed; so too the rich man in the midst of his pursuits will fade away.

Rare and scarce,
precious and priceless,
inestimable and invaluable.
These are just a few words which describe that desirable attribute, that much sought after virtue which men call wisdom. The English poet Samuel Taylor Coleridge once wrote, "Common sense in an uncommon degree

is what the world calls wisdom." Webster puts it this way, "Wisdom is the quality of being wise; it is knowledge with capacity to use it; it is the perception of the best ends and the best means."[1]

Wisdom is that virtue which enables a man to make decisions as God would make them. Putting it another way, a wise man is one who solves his problems in the same manner as God would solve them.

VERSE 5

James discusses this matter of the Christian and his problem of having wisdom. He calls attention to three very fundamental considerations: the need for wisdom, the source of wisdom and the availability of wisdom.

Need for Wisdom

In a subtle, soft-sell approach, James points out a definite need in the life of every man for wisdom. Focus for a moment on the small word *any* in verse 5. Even though it has only three letters, it refers to men and women from all walks of life. Both the highly educated and those who have no training at all in the intellectual disciplines are included in it. Both the rich and the poor are described by it. Without exception every man, woman and child is covered by it. James is saying that no man—regardless of how learned or how rich or how prominent he may be—can make it in life unless he is a wise man, a man who can solve his problems as God would solve them.

There is a vast difference between knowledge and wisdom. Even a casual observance of what is taking place today reveals the truth of this. The advancement

Wisdom—true wisdom, wisdom that emanates from God—is available to man.

of technology has made a great impact on the education of today's youth. Because of the tremendous emphasis on formal education both in this country and around the world, students of all ages have more information at their command than those of previous generations.

In spite of this vast and increasing storehouse of knowledge, man is witnessing a retrogression of morality and ethics such as the world has never seen. Increased knowledge has been of no help whatsoever as far as this basic problem is concerned. One commentator wrote, "Through knowledge man has learned to travel faster than sound but shows his lack of wisdom by going faster in the wrong direction."[2] Charles Haddon Spurgeon had it right when he said, "Wisdom is the right use of knowledge. To know is not to be wise. Many men know a great deal and are all the greater fools for it. There is no fool so great a fool as a knowing fool. But to know how to use knowledge is to have wisdom."

Source of Wisdom

James turns his attention from the need for wisdom to the source of wisdom, which is Almighty God. In seeking the source of wisdom, the old patriarch Job cries out, "But where can wisdom be found?" (Job 28:12.)

His answer is that wisdom is not found among the living on earth, it is not found in the depths of the sea, it cannot be purchased with gold and it cannot be bought with precious stones. Finally he declared, "Behold, the fear of the Lord, that is wisdom (Job 28:28). True wisdom has its source in the living God.

Wisdom—true wisdom, wisdom that emanates from

God—is available to man. Just think of it! God makes available to us the ability to solve problems just as He would solve them. Everyone can become a wise person.

VERSES 6, 7, 8
Available Wisdom

True wisdom is available to man through prayer. One day David found himself involved in a battle with the Philistines in the Valley of Rephaim. God instructed David to encircle the enemy and come in from behind at the point where the mulberry trees were located. He was told that when he heard a stirring in those trees, he was to begin the attack. This he did, carrying out God's counsel to the letter. As a result he won an overwhelming victory (see 2 Samuel 5:22).

Close scrutiny of David's life reveals that the only time he got into difficulty was when he tried to handle his own problems without guidance from the Lord.

By inference and by direct statement, James sets forth two requirements which must be met by the individual before God will answer his prayers and give him the wisdom he desires.

The first requirement, based entirely on inference, is that to receive the wisdom of God through prayer a person must be a Christian. This is seen more clearly when considering the people to whom the book of James is addressed. He wrote to Christians. James had believers in mind.

The second requirement is spelled out: Pray with faith. Several things happen to the person who does not have faith when he prays. This person is driven and tossed with the wind. His prayer will not be answered.

He is called a double-minded man and is considered unstable in all his ways. The word *double-minded* is the Greek word, *dipsuchos,* which literally means a man with two souls. One soul believes, the other disbelieves. This word actually pictures a man who has a civil war going on continually inside of him.

In this passage, James 1:5-11, the Holy Spirit through James gives a twofold assurance—one a positive assurance and the other a negative.

Positively speaking James says that when Christians pray in faith for wisdom, it will be given liberally. Christians will be able to solve problems completely and perfectly just as God Himself would solve them. A Baptist pastor was invited to speak at an open forum in a Reformed Jewish synagogue. His assigned subject was, "Why I Believe the Bible to Be the Word of God." He spoke on this subject for an hour and 10 minutes. Following his message the meeting was opened for questions. The first one asked was, "Can a Jew be saved without accepting Jesus Christ as Lord and Savior?" The response was, "Let's not put this on a racial basis. The Bible teaches that no one can be saved without committing himself in faith to Christ."

This caused a stir through the entire Jewish section of the congregation. One who was especially angered stood up and said, "Let all of us who are Jews go home. We are going to hell, anyway, because the pastor has the keys to heaven in his pocket." Quietly the pastor bowed his head and asked the Lord for wisdom. Immediately God answered. Holding his Bible up the pastor said, "No, my friend, I don't have the keys to heaven in my pocket. I have them in my hand. My prayer is that you will find them there just as I did. If you so desire, I shall be glad to help you in the search."

Negatively speaking James says that when Christians pray in faith asking for wisdom, God will not upbraid them. God is their heavenly Father and as such is perfect. He is not like the daddy of the little boy who became irritated because the child asked him twice to help him with a homework assignment. In exasperation he said to his son, "Use your own common sense and figure it out for yourself." God wants to be bothered. It is His desire that Christians ask for what they need.

Yes, it is true! If any Christian lacks wisdom, he may ask God for it in faith and the results will be most gratifying. God will not upbraid him. Instead He will give it to him liberally.

This wisdom is to be used in every area of the Christian life. In the rest of this chapter, James illustrates this concept by indicating the danger of placing one's confidence in material things.

Wealth

James recognized that there were economic distinctions within the membership of the church. He addressed verse 9 to those who are poor, and verses 10-11, the affluent. It is most significant to note that James did not consider these economic differences as constituting a problem that the church had to solve. Neither in this passage nor in any other throughout the book did he suggest a program of redistributing the wealth so that each member might have a like amount.

James was no socialist. He was a realist. He recognized that God had endowed men with varying degrees of ability to acquire material possessions. His concern was that the two, the rich and the poor, might exist harmoniously together within the church because of their common faith in and love for Jesus Christ. He knew that each had a worthy contribution to make to the Savior's program.

VERSE 9

James has a special message for Christians of moderate or less than moderate circumstances.

The small word *let* does not introduce a request but a command. James is not requesting that the Christians in the lower economic bracket do something; he is demanding it.

A paraphrase of this is, "Almighty God demands that you Christians who have not risen very far above the ground financially, you that are of moderate or less-than-moderate circumstances boast loudly about the fact that He has exalted you. You have every right to be proud of this."

Attitude of the Poor

Several important truths appear in this paraphrase. Every believer, regardless of his financial position, has been exalted by Almighty God. When a man turns in faith to Jesus Christ, his bank account, real estate holdings and stocks and bonds are not checked in order to ascertain whether or not he is eligible to become a Christian. Instead, by the power of the Holy Spirit he is immediately made a new creation in Christ Jesus. He becomes a member of God's family and a citizen in His kingdom. From then on he does not have to concern himself about what the future holds because he has an intimate personal relationship with the One who holds the future.

In this verse James teaches that every believer has both the right and the responsibility of boasting about God's giving him a position of exaltation. The reason for this is obvious. When the Christian boasts in this manner, others hear him and wonder if God will do the same for them. This opens the door to the Christian for witnessing. It gives him an opportunity to influence others to make the decision for the Savior that he has made. It enables him to literally carry out the Great Commission.

No Christian has a right to feel sorry for himself when he is confronted with financial difficulty. Unfortunately there are many people today who say they love Christ, but when they find themselves financially embarrassed they get down in the mouth and bitter. They become so negative and disgruntled that it is almost impossible to live with them.

VERSES 10, 11

As James thought about the church of his day, he realized that not all of the members were in moderate circumstances. There were some like Joseph of Arimathea, Nicodemus and Barnabas who were exceedingly rich. These men had been most successful in the acquisition of material possessions. In these verses James addressed a special message to them and to affluent believers of every generation. Consider carefully his message. There are two parts to it. First, a command which the wealthy Christian is to implement in his life; second, reasons why he is to do this.

Attitude of the Rich

The command is at the beginning of verse 10. The rich Christian is told to glory in the fact that his material possessions mean nothing to his eternal salvation. He dares not trust in riches because money and possessions don't last. The rich man approaches God empty-handed. With humility he accepts God's gift of Jesus Christ. He knows his dependence for redemption is not on money but on Jesus.

The rich man, like the poor, is ever confronted with the prospect of death. The truth is that money at the time of death does an individual no good whatsoever. Someone asked concerning a wealthy man, "How much did he leave?" The answer was, "He left it all. There are no pockets in shrouds."

The only thing that really counts at the time of death is one's right relationship to God through Jesus Christ. The rich Christian as well as the poor can rejoice not only that he knows the truth of this, but also that he has based his eternal future on that truth.

FOR REFLECTION

How does the wise Christian solve his problems?

Compare the demand James makes of the financially poor Christian with his demand of the wealthy Christian.

Footnotes

1. *Webster's Seventh New Collegiate Dictionary* (Springfield: G. & C. Merriam Company, Publishers, 1967).
2. Lehman Strauss, *James, Your Brother* (New York: Loizeaux Brothers, 1956), p. 19.

CHAPTER THREE

SAY NO!

JAMES 1:13-15

JAMES 1:13-15

13. Let no one say when he is tempted, "I am being tempted by God;" for God cannot be tempted by evil, and He Himself does not tempt any one.
14. But each one is tempted when he is carried away and enticed by his own lust.
15. Then when lust has conceived, it gives birth to sin; and when sin is accomplished, it brings forth death.

The historical backdrop against which this Epistle was written is important. The writer James, son of Mary and Joseph, was a Jew. He was writing to the Christians scattered throughout the then known world. Most of these had been converted from Judaism. This means that both James and the people to whom he was writing were familiar with basic Jewish teaching, including the origin of evil. Like everyone else, the Jews were troubled about the problem of how sin got into the human race. Through the years their scholars struggled with this problem until they finally hit upon a solution which was satisfactory to at least most of their leaders.

Origin of Sin

The struggle began with the assumption that within every man a continual civil war is taking place. Without exception every individual has within him two tendencies or two natures which are everlastingly contending with one another and simultaneously pulling him in opposite directions. The good nature within man the Jewish scholars called *yetser hatob*, and the evil nature *yetser hara*. *Yetser hatob* and *yetser hara* like two dogs—the good dog and the bad dog—were constantly at one another's throats.

As the leaders of Judaism continued through the years in their struggle to solve the problem of the origin of evil, several theories were developed. There were those who believed that evil originated with Satan. Others contended that the fallen angels were responsible for it. Some felt that man himself was the reason for it.

As the rabbis examined these theories they were convinced that none was correct. They argued that Satan may have put it into man, but who put it into Satan? The fallen angels may have put it into man, but who put it into the angels? Man may have put it into himself, but where did it ultimately come from?

In order to solve this problem, the rabbis took a very bold and irrational step. They contended that only God could have created the evil tendency in man. By so doing they made God, who is absolute purity, the author of evil.

VERSE 13

James recognized that many of these Christians who had been converted out of Judaism might have a tendency to blame God when confronted by temptation to do evil.

The inconspicuous preposition *of* in the phrase "tempted of God" *(KJV)* is important. In the Greek language there are two words which are translated *of.* One

Through the presence of the Holy Spirit the Christian has the power to hold in subjection and to restrict that natural bent to do wrong.

is the word *hupo* and the other is the word *apo*. There is as vast difference in these two words. The preposition *hupo* when used with a proper name would imply a direct assault. If it were used in this passage with the name *God*, it would picture God approaching the person face-to-face, taking him by the hand and actually leading him to do evil. This is not the word that is used, however.

The fixing of blame on God is a far more subtle proposition brought out by the word *apo*. It has the idea of God being responsible for the temptation, indirectly, either through circumstances or environment or perhaps another person whom He brings into the individual's life. Dr. Spiros Zodhiates explains the reasoning of this kind of man, "God has ordained that I should yield to the temptation under which I have fallen. I have been driven to sin, not by God himself since He hates sin, but by the very circumstances in which God has placed me. God is the ultimate cause and therefore I should absolve myself of the responsibility." Dr. Zodhiates then adds, "The position of man seems to be quite plausible, doesn't it? But remember that with God's eternal providence and purposes there coexists man's moral freedom, and in this moral freedom must lie the responsibility of man."[1]

Keeping this in mind look at the second part of verse 13. In it is the reason why man should never blame God for the temptations that come his way. God does not tempt anyone.

Tempting God

James explains that God cannot be tempted in the sense that He will yield to the temptation and become involved experientially with the evil that it seeks to bring. The reason that the Scriptures reveal for this is that God is absolute and perfect holiness. Instead of tempting man, God seeks to get him in his daily life to emulate the example of the Lord Jesus Christ.

There is a natural tendency on everyone's part to blame someone else and ultimately God for his being tempted to sin. Verse 13 shows it is God's will for all Christians to take the responsibility for the evil which they commit. In mercy God has provided a way by which forgiveness is available. That way is both clearly outlined and illustrated in 1 John 1:9. When a believer commits a sin, he does not have to fear God if he carries out the instructions of this verse. He only has to fear Him when he tries to pass the buck, when he tries to blame someone else for his wrongdoing.

A Southern governor visited the inmates of the state penitentiary. As he talked to one after another, he heard excuse piled upon excuse as to why these men were behind bars. Some blamed their predicament on the environment in which they grew up. Others attributed their incarceration to the fact that they had never had a chance to get an education. Still others blamed their difficulties on getting in with the wrong companions.

Finally the governor visited a young man who said in response to the question of why he was in prison, "I am here because I broke the law. It is no one's fault but my own. I am paying my debt to society and I trust that someday I shall be forgiven for my wrongdoing."

When the governor returned to his office, he wrote out a pardon for this young man. To it he appended a personal note which said, "I am pardoning John because I don't want him to stay in that prison and corrupt all of those innocent people."

VERSE 14

James explains that the source of man's temptation to do evil is not God, but rather man himself. The lust within man tends to involve him in compromising situations. Often it drives him to do that which is completely antithetical to God's will for his life.

Sin's Attraction

In order to understand what is involved in this, consider the sinfulness of man's nature and the attractiveness of sin. Every man has within him a tendency to do evil. The Christian may object and say, "But when I became a Christian wasn't my natural inclination to do evil destroyed?" The answer is absolutely no! It is true that Christ's righteousness is imputed to the Christian. This does not mean, however, that the evil tendency was destroyed. Through the presence of the Holy Spirit the Christian has the power to hold in subjection and to restrict that natural bent to do wrong.

The attractiveness of sin is real. It is exceedingly alluring and enticing. Like fool's gold, it glitters on the surface. When man fixes his gaze upon it and begins to rationalize about it, temptation to sin becomes a living, pulsating, driving reality in his life.

VERSE 15

The progression of evil is described in three downward steps. First, there is the lust or the temptation. Then there is the yielding to this temptation. The third step is death.

William Shakespeare in his immortal tragedy *Mac-*

beth has illustrated the three retrogressive steps of evil in Lady Macbeth. This lady had set her eyes upon becoming Queen of Scotland. The one thing standing between her and the realization of her ambition was her husband's kinsman, Duncan, the present king. So great was her desire to be queen that it motivated her to plot the murder of Duncan and then to persuade her husband to carry it out.

She arranged what appeared to be the perfect murder. There was just one little fly in the ointment. She had to live with herself. In the most tragic scene of the play she comes on stage walking in her sleep, crying, "Out, damned spot! Out I say!" And then she shrieks, "All the perfumes of Arabia will not sweeten this little hand."[2]

First, there was lust. Second, lust resulted in sin. Third, sin spawned death—the death of Lady Macbeth's happiness and the death of her usefulness. Her story is the story of every human being who yields to the lust of the flesh.

Fighting Temptation

What can Christians do to withstand the daily temptations to do evil? There are very practical suggestions given in the Bible. After Jesus had finished praying in the garden of Gethsemane for the first time, He went back to where Peter, James and John were supposed to by praying. He found them asleep. He rebuked them for this saying, "Keep watching and praying, that you may not enter into temptation" (Matt. 26:41). Implicit in this command is the idea that Christians are to use their will-power to fight against these things.

Jesus not only said, "Watch," He also said, "Pray." If every time an individual is tempted to do evil, he stops and asks God's help in withstanding that temptation, he will have less difficulty in emerging triumphant over it. The problem usually is that man goes ahead, gets involved and then finds himself confronted with the necessity of asking for forgiveness. While he can be grateful that the Lord is always ready to forgive, it would be far better if he would pray and avoid yielding in the first place.

The apostle Paul says again and again when facing temptation to concentrate upon Jesus. William Barclay summarized this idea accurately, "The Christian can so hand himself over to Christ and to the Spirit of Christ that he is cleansed of evil desire. He can be so engaged in good things that there is no time or place left for wrong desires. It is idle hands for which Satan finds mischief to do. It is an unexercised mind which plays with desire and an uncommitted heart which is vulnerable to the appeal of lust."[3]

FOR REFLECTION

Where is the source of evil according to the Hebrew rabbis? _____ *according to James?* _____
List three ways a Christian can fight temptation.

Footnotes

1. Spiros Zodhiates, *The Work of Faith* (Grand Rapids: Wm. B. Eerdmans Publishing Co.). Used by permission.
2. William Shakespeare, *Macbeth*, Act V, Sc. 1, Line 38 and line 56.
3. *The Letters of James and Peter*, translated and interpreted by William Barclay. Published by the Saint Andrew Press, Edinburgh, 1958; and in the U.S.A. by the Westminster Press, 1961, p. 61.

CHAPTER FOUR

GATEWAY TO FREEDOM

JAMES 1:16-27

JAMES 1:16-27

16. Do not be deceived, my beloved brethren.
17. Every good thing bestowed and every perfect gift is from above, coming down from the Father of lights, with whom there is no variation, or shifting shadow.
18. In the exercise of His will He brought us forth by the word of truth, so that we might be as it were the first fruits among His creatures.
19. *This* you know, my beloved brethren. But let every one be quick to hear, slow to speak *and* slow to anger;
20. for the anger of man does not achieve the righteousness of God.
21. Therefore putting aside all filthiness and *all* that remains of wickedness, in humility receive the word implanted, which is able to save your souls.
22. But prove yourselves doers of the word, and not merely hearers who delude themselves.
23. For if any one is a hearer of the word and not a doer, he is like a man who looks at his natural face in a mirror;
24. for *once* he has looked at himself and gone away, he has immediately forgotten what kind of person he was.
25. But one who looks intently at the perfect law, the *law* of liberty and abides by it, not having

become a forgetful hearer but an effectual doer, this man shall be blessed in what he does.

26. If any one thinks himself to be religious, and yet does not bridle his tongue but deceived his *own* heart, this man's religion is worthless.

27. This is pure and undefiled religion in the sight of .our God and Father, to visit orphans and . widows in their distress, *and* to keep oneself unstained by the world.

VERSES 16, 17

Be sure to notice the word *good* in verse 17. It was used long ago to describe the birth of a king or a nobleman. Such a person was said to have a good birth in that he came from royal parentage. If effect James is saying that every gift that originally comes from God is good. The subtle implication James makes here is that while everything God gives to man originally is good, man often takes these good things, misuses them and thereby turns them into evil.

The word translated as *perfect* in the phrase "every perfect gift" is the Greek word *telos,* which has the idea of purpose connected with it. Every gift that God gives is perfect in the sense that it has purpose to it—a purpose which God wants to see accomplished either in or through a person's life.

The gift God gives may be something desirable from the human point of view. For example He may give him the ability of making money. When he does, wise is that man who realizes that God has a purpose in this to the extent that he give 90 percent of his income to the

Lord's work while keeping only 10 percent for himself.

Source of Blessing

There are no exceptions to the central truth that God is the source of all blessings. The word *every* at the beginning of verse 17 is all-inclusive. It includes all that people are prone to take for granted, as well as the unusual blessings. It includes food, clothes, air, health, home, cars and loving friends.

Although God is Himself changeless, unvarying in His character, He has created the many variations of the sun, moon, stars and their galaxies. The sun appears to be closer to the earth at certain times during the year. Sometimes the sun is totally eclipsed by the moon. The stars and galaxies move about in outer space. Unlike the heavenly lights which He has created, God is unchangeable. With Him there is no variation or shifting. He is always the same.

VERSE 18

God, the source of all blessings, offers every individual the new birth experience by His Holy Spirit. In the exercise of His will, God made man's redemption a reality by the Word of truth, the Savior. Christians are the "first fruits among His creatures."

The term *firstfruits* is best understood in the light of the Old Testament teaching that the firstfruits of each harvest belonged to God. They were His particular possession. And so it is with Christians. They belong to God, are His *firstfruits* and are uniquely His possessions. He created them and, through the new birth, He re-created them. Christians are twice His.

Six Commands

God's expectation for a Christian's life is spelled out specifically. Six practical commands are listed and partially illustrated in the remaining part of this first chapter.

These commands are simply stated:

Be quick to hear;

Be slow to speak;

Be slow to anger;

Set aside filthiness and wickedness;

Receive the Word of God in your life;

Become involved as a doer in the work of the Lord Jesus Christ.

VERSES 19, 20
Quick to Hear

Christians may express gratitude to God for His multiple blessings by being quick to hear Him. James says they are to be swift, quick to take advantage of every opportunity to hear the Word of God. God speaks today through His ministers, competent Bible teachers, Christ-centered literature and through the Holy Spirit's interpreting the Scriptures to those who hear, read and study them. In this first command to be quick to hear, James explains the need for people to avail themselves of all avenues of learning and to saturate their minds with spiritual knowledge.

Slow to Speak

Specifically, the command, "Be ... slow to speak," teaches that a Christian should be slow to speak publicly concerning the great doctrines of the faith. Only after spending hours in intensive study should a Christian undertake publicly the expounding of the profound truths of the Word of God. Don't forget! God trained Moses 80 years for 40 years of service. He gave well-educated Paul three years of additional special preparation out in the Arabian desert before He allowed him to become the flaming apostle to the Gentiles.

Slow to Anger

The command to be slow to anger implies a slowness to express wrath, and it also implies a time when wrath is in keeping with the will of God. This type of wrath is usually termed righteous indignation.

There were times in the life of Jesus when His actions were motivated by righteous indignation. In justifiable anger He cleansed the Temple of the money-changers and merchandisers (see Matt. 21:12-13). Jesus did not hesitate to speak what was on His mind to the Jewish religious leaders of His day. A scathing denunciation of the scribes and Pharisees is recorded in Matthew 23.

Set Aside Filthiness

James says the man who really appreciates the blessings of God will demonstrate it by eliminating those sins and vices that destroy his effectiveness as a witness for Christ.

One day a preacher visited a coal-mining town and noticed how dingy it was. The coal dust seemed to blacken the buildings, the trees, the shrubs and everything else. As he was walking down the street with the foreman of the mine, his attention was captivated by a beautiful, white flower. He commented, "The owner of this flower surely must take care of it. There's no dust and dirt on it at all."

The foreman threw a handful of dust on the flower. It immediately fell off and left the flower as stainless as before. "It has a natural enamel which prevents any dust from clinging to it," the foreman explained. "I think it must have been created especially for such a place as this."

Surely this is the way Christians are to be in the midst of a world that is filthy because of the dust and dirt of sin. God gives a spiritual enamel to those who yield themselves completely to the leadership of the Holy Spirit and who seek to make Christ Lord of their lives.

VERSE 21

The key to understanding this command in verse 21 is found in the word *implanted.* The seed of the gospel is planted in the hearts of all who are Christians the moment Jesus Christ takes possessions of their lives. The Christian is to receive this seed and cultivate it, giving it a chance to grow to maturity.

When considering the first and fifth commands together, James says those who have already received the seed of the gospel are to take advantage of every opportunity presented them to learn more about spiritual truth.

Become Involved

The final command for daily living is to be active in the work of Jesus Christ. One of the most serious problems

Christians must realize that the secret to real and abiding happiness is found in selfless, daily service to the Savior.

facing the church right now can be summarized in one word: _unwillingness_. A great majority of the people who say they love Jesus Christ are unwilling to demonstrate it by their actions. They attend services when it is convenient; they accept God's blessing in their lives. But they adamantly refuse to become involved in His work. This unwilling spirit on the part of many Christians is really just a reflection of life in general today. It mirrors the mood and temper of our times.

Someone in an effort to point out the complete absurdity of our modern don't-get-involved philosophy has imagined what some of the great heroes of our country might have said following this line of reasoning:

Nathan Hale—Me spy on the British? You've got to be kidding! You know what they do to spies? I'll tell you, man. They hang 'em. I just can't afford to take the risk.

Paul Revere—What do you mean, ride through every Middlesex village and town, and in the middle of the night? Why pick on me? Am I the only man in Boston with a horse?

Patrick Henry—Sure, I'm for liberty. But let's be a little realistic. We're a pretty small outfit. If we start kicking up a fuss with the British, somebody's going to get hurt. I just can't stand to be hurt. I can't stand to be alone on any issue.

George Washington—Gentlemen, I am honored. But I do wish you would try someone else. I'm just getting things organized at Mount Vernon. I have so many things that I need to be doing at home. And, after all, you know I don't get to spend much time with my family. Anyway, I have already fought against the French.

Benjamin Franklin—What we really need as an ambassador to France is a young man. It's time a new generation took over.

VERSE 22
Self-deception

A young minister preached his first sermon in the church to which he had been called. It was well received and the people expressed their appreciation as they shook his hand at the door of the sanctuary. The next Sunday the young man preached the same sermon. He continued to preach it for the following three Sundays.

Finally his board of deacons met and inquired whether or not he had any other sermons. When he said yes, they asked why he kept repeating the first sermon. He asked them, "Have you put into practice the first one I preached?" They admitted they hadn't. "Why should I preach another until the first really means something to you in terms of your everyday experiences?" he asked. They were embarrassed and had no answer.

James emphasizes that the Christians who are hearers only of God's Word are actually guilty of self-deception. *Hearer* comes from the Greek word *akroatai* meaning those who listen attentively with a real interest in what is being said. It is a word used to describe an auditor in a university. The auditor has no responsibility as far as the classes are concerned and when graduation comes, he is without recognition.

VERSES 23, 24

In these verses James pictures the Christian who is a hearer of the word but not a doer. He is like a man who looks in a mirror and sees all of his imperfections. He notices his crooked tie, his uncombed hair, his grimy face, soiled shirt and dirty glasses. Instead of taking care of himself, he goes on his way, forgetting all about the problems and continuing to present a most unattractive appearance.

So it is with the believer who hears without doing. He repels people from the Savior rather than drawing them to Him. He is looked upon by those outside of Christ as a hypocrite.

VERSE 25
Mature Christian

The next picture James draws is God's concept of the mature Christian. The word *looks* in this verse comes from the Greek word *parakuptoo*, meaning "to stoop down." The full-grown Christian is one who stoops down or one who humbles himself before the Word of God. He studies it, meditates upon it and absorbs it, letting it actually become a part of him. In this way he has an intimate and personal fellowship with the Lord Jesus Christ.

Christians must realize that the secret to real and abiding happiness is found in selfless, daily service to the Savior.

VERSE 26

If a man seems religious and does not bridle or control his tongue, James says two things happen. He deceives himself no matter how outwardly religious he is. And his religion is vain and worthless as far as making any real contribution to the cause of Christ is concerned. He is a stumbling block in the Savior's program rather than a stepping-stone.

VERSE 27

James expresses the basic idea of this verse by saying that a part of pure and undefiled religion is for the believer to keep himself unspotted from the world. God wants only clear and pure vessels in His service. Those Christians who are constantly playing footsie with the world, compromising their convictions, are of little use to the Savior.

FOR REFLECTION

List the six commands for a Christian life on a sheet of paper. Beside each command write one goal for self-improvement to work on this week.

What is the difference between the mature Christian and the auditor?

CHAPTER FIVE

RICH MAN, POOR MAN

JAMES 2:1-13

JAMES 2:1-13

1. My brethren, do not hold your faith in our glorious Lord Jesus Christ with an *attitude of* personal favoritism.
2. For if a man comes into your assembly with a gold ring and dressed in fine clothes, and there also comes in a poor man in dirty clothes,
3. and you pay special attention to the one who is wearing the fine clothes, and say, "You sit here in a good place," and you say to the poor man, "You stand over there, or sit down by my footstool",
4. have you not made distinctions among yourselves, and become judges with evil motives?
5. Listen, my beloved brethren: did not God choose the poor of this world *to be* rich in faith, and heirs of the kingdom which He promised to those who love Him?
6. But you have dishonored the poor man. Is it not the rich who oppress you and personally drag you into court?
7. Do they not blaspheme the fair name by which you have been called?
8. If, however, you are fulfilling the royal law, according to the Scriptures "You shall love your neighbor as yourself," you are doing well.

9. But if you show partiality, you are committing sin *and* are convicted by the law as transgressors.

10. For whoever keeps the whole law and yet stumbles in one *point* he has become guilty of all.

11. For He who said, "Do not commit adultery," also said, "do not commit murder." Now if you do not commit adultery, but do commit murder, you have become a transgressor of the law.

12. So speak and so act, as those who are to be judged by *the* law of liberty.

13. For judgment *will be* merciless to one who has shown no mercy; mercy triumphs over judgment.

VERSE 1

Close to the top of a list of the most prevalent sins in the church today is the sin which the Bible calls *respect of persons (KJV)*. In some modern versions it is translated as *snobbery*. Actually it is the sin of giving preferential treatment within the church to an individual simply because he may have money or may be successful in his business or profession. So commonplace is the sin within churches that those who give this preferential treatment seem to know no other course of action and those who receive it have come to expect it.

James recognized that the respect of persons is a deadly sin. He instructs the people in his church in Jerusalem—and through them the members of all churches—to deal with their fellowman on the basis of the well-established biblical principle that God is no respecter of persons (see Acts 10:34). He points out that whether or not people are actually Christians can be determined in part by the way in which they deal with their fellowmen.

This point is brought out clearly by two modern writers. Barclay puts it this way: "My brothers, you cannot really believe that you have faith in our glorious Lord Jesus Christ, and yet continue to have respect of person." Kenneth Taylor paraphrases the verse, "Dear Brothers, how can you claim that you belong to the Lord Jesus Christ, the Lord of glory, if you show favoritism to rich people and look down on poor people?" (TLB).

The questions that each person should ask himself are: "How does my Christianity measure up in the light of this very practical test? Do both God and my neighbors see me showing love and respect for all men regardless of their position in life?"

Witnessing

The most valuable commodity in all the world is the human soul. Much thought and much time should be given to witnessing to those who are outside of Christ. Most people are busy. They have social obligations and responsibilities at home, church and work. After acknowledging all of this, ask yourself this question, "Would I like to see one of my friends in hell simply because I was too busy to tell him the story of redemption?" There was time to go to parties with him and time to play golf with him and help in civic programs with him, but no time to tell him about Jesus. What a tragedy!

VERSES 2, 3, 4
Rich/Poor Man

In verses 2-4 James uses a parable to illustrate the way respect of persons often works in the church: The first man in verse 2 is exceedingly wealthy. He is described as wearing a gold ring and dressed in goodly or expensive apparel. In the original Greek the word translated *ring* is in the plural. He may be pictured as one who had rings on practically every finger. It is significant to note this because in New Testament times rings were a sign of great affluence.

The second man in this story is a very poor man. This is evidenced by the fact that he is dressed in dirty clothes. The word *dirty* is the Greek word *rupara* and it means filthy and unclean. This man is most unattractive. There is a stench about him. He is like the bum who stumbles into a rescue mission on skid row looking for a doughnut and a cup of coffee.

As these two men, the rich and the poor, come into the church service together, immediately the usher commits the sin of respect of persons. He gives preferential treatment to the wealthy man by showing him to the choicest seat in the sanctuary while telling the poor man that he could either stand up during the service or sit on the floor.

The early church had a real problem at this point, and churches through the years have had to face it. Even a casual reading of church history reveals that the church was often guilty of awarding its positions of authority and esteem to an individual, not on the basis of spiritual maturity, but rather on the basis of his ability and willingness to pay for the position.

The sin of respect of persons is so prevalent in

The reason most people commit the sin of respect of persons is that they have an erroneous sense of values.

churches today that it is not recognized as a serious problem. Instead, it is too often merely a subject of humor.

A woman who lived across the tracks wanted to join a very fashionable downtown church. She talked to the pastor about it and he suggested she go home and think about it carefully for a week. At the end of the week she came back. He said, "Now, let's not be hasty. Go home and read your Bible for an hour every day this week. Then come back and tell me if you feel you should join." Although she wasn't happy about this, she agreed to do it. The next week she was back, assuring the pastor she wanted to become a member of the church.

In exasperation he said, "I have one more suggestion. You pray every day this week and ask the Lord if He wants you to come into our fellowship." The pastor did not see the woman for six months. He met her on the street one day and asked her what she had decided. She said, "I did what you asked me to do. I went home and prayed. One day while I was praying, the Lord said to me, 'Don't worry about not getting into that church. I've been trying to get into it Myself for the last 20 years and haven't made it.'"

An aside here—this parable includes an intimation that Christians, in order to maintain a maximum testimony for Christ, should dress in a modest or discreet manner. The ring worn by the rich man in the parable is not too important per se. Neither is his bright apparel. It is the principle behind these things which is important. The principle is that modesty in dress is a great virtue which every Christian should exemplify. Most Christians do not often overdress to display their wealth. This does not mean, however, that Christians do not have a problem as far as modesty in dress is concerned in this sex-crazy age. The world, the flesh and the devil have combined talents to pressurize Christian people into letting the bars down as far as clothing is concerned. Like it or not, these worldly standards are having bad effects in Christian circles.

Now getting back to the parable—James is not teaching that to be wealthy is sinful. The rich man who came to the same church service as the man dressed in dirty clothes was not condemned because of his affluence. The sin of giving greater respect to the rich man was committed by the usher. Nowhere in the Scriptures is it taught that a man possessing money is a sinner simply because he has it. The sin connected with money is in misusing it.

When a man gets to the place where the accumulation of money becomes his magnificent obsession in life, then he is guilty of the sin of idolatry. He is actually worshiping filthy lucre. However, when a man uses his money to the glory of God, not thinking of himself, he does that which is well pleasing to the Lord. He is an obedient servant.

James draws attention to the fact that the reason most people commit the sin of respect of persons is that they have an erroneous sense of values. This is made clear in verses 3 and 4. The usher in the story showed the rich man preferential treatment because he was judging by false standards. Money is no index to the worth of anyone.

Man's Value

How much is a person worth? No one actually knows. Only God can answer this question. And the Almighty is going to answer it eternally for each person. The Bible unequivocally teaches (see Matt. 24:45-51; 25:14-30; Luke 19:11-27; John 14:1-6; Acts 16:31) that His answer for every individual is based on two considerations. Has the person received God's gift of eternal redemption, which He has offered through the crucifixion, resurrection, intercession and return of His beloved Son? Has the person after receiving His gift of salvation been faithful in serving the Savior with time, capabilities and income?

If the person sincerely and honestly answers the first question in the affirmative then he has personal assurance from God that he is of infinite value in His sight. So much so that He has prepared an eternal abode for him in His own heavenly home. If the person sincerely and honestly answers yes to the second question, once again he has assurance from God that his worth to Him is invaluable. In addition to the heavenly home which God will give, He has provided rewards for him which are beyond man's vocabulary to describe.

VERSE 5

James states a paradox of Christianity in the form of a question. The concept in this verse—namely, that God really loves the poor—was completely contrary to the opinion held by most of the people in New Testament days.

It wasn't until after the Holy Spirit came upon the disciples at Pentecost that they really understood that salvation is for everyone. Salvation is for the rich and the poor, the Jew and the Gentile, the cultured and the uncultured and the educated and the uneducated. James recognized the truth of this. He was aware that for the most part it was the poor who had responded in the affirmative to the invitation of the Savior.

The apostle Paul agreed with James in 1 Corinthians 1:26-29. William Barclay commented on this passage, "It is not that Christ and the church do not want the great and the rich and the wise and the mighty; we must be aware of an inverted snobbery, as we have already seen. But it was the simple fact that the gospel offered so much to the poor, and demanded so much from the rich, that it was the poor who were swept into the church. It was, in fact, the common people who heard Jesus gladly, and the rich young ruler who went sorrowfully away because he had great possessions."[2]

A famous and wealthy English noblewoman, in talking about 1 Corinthians 1:26 said one letter made it possible for her to follow Christ. It was the letter *m*. Paul said, "Not many wise . . . mighty . . . noble." Without the *m* the statement would have read, "Not any . . . wise mighty . . . noble."

VERSES 6, 7

James speaks directly to the usher who was guilty of this sin of favoritism, the one who gave preferential treatment to the rich visitor who came into the service. James said to that man, "You have dishonored the poor man."

Two Questions

James then asks the usher two questions. First, "Is it not the rich who oppress you and personally drag you into court?" This question refers to a custom which was practiced daily in the society of which he was a part. It was the custom of summary arrest. A rich man would meet a poor man on the street who owed him money. He would seize him by the neck of his robe, drawing it tight so that he nearly strangled him. He would then literally drag him into a court of law where the poor man was required to explain why he had been unable to meet his financial obligations. If he could not give a satisfactory explanation, he was cast into prison where he remained until his debts were paid.

James then asked, "Do they not blaspheme the fair name by which you have been called?" The word which James uses for *called* is the Greek word *epikaleisthai*. It is the word used when a wife takes her husband's name or a child his father's name. When a person accepts Jesus Christ as Savior, he takes the worthy name of Christian. In this question, James points out that the rich were in the habit of blaspheming that name.

This is how it would happen. A slave of a wealthy owner would be converted. From that moment on he was a better slave in the sense that he did his work more efficiently. However, he would not be party to his master's dishonest deals. When the master threatened him for this, he would not be intimidated. Being a Christian, he insisted on having time off on the Lord's Day for public worship. Naturally all of this infuriated the wealthy owner and resulted in his blaspheming the name of Christ.

In raising these two questions with the usher, James was in no sense censuring the wealthy for their possession of money. He was not implying that they were inherently evil because of their affluence. Instead, he was chiding them both for their oppression of those who were poverty-stricken and for their failure to consider them as human beings whom God loves.

Before leaving this section dealing with the paradox of the Christian faith, there is one more great truth to be found. James says even though a man may be poor as far as his monetary resources are concerned, if he has Jesus Christ as Savior, he is both rich in faith and is an heir of the kingdom which God has promised to those who love Him.

How reassuring and exciting this is! It is the most comforting truth which the Bible reveals.

VERSE 8

James turns to a most important pronouncement concerning the Christian in his relationship to the Law. James is speaking directly to the usher. He points out two ways open to every Christian in which he may treat other people. He may treat them in the godly way or in the ungodly way.

Royal Law

There is a great urgency in the heart of James as he writes verse 8. The key word in understanding this statement is *fulfill*. It comes from the Greek verb *teleite* which means "to bring to a place of perfection or completeness." What a beautiful thought James is suggesting here. The moment a Christian accepts Christ, he is entrusted with the love of God. It is his responsibility to bring this love to completion in this world by loving his neighbor as himself.

In the story of the good Samaritan, Jesus defines a neighbor as anyone in need whether friend or foe (see Luke 10:25-37). It is easy to love the one who is lovely and loves in return. It is difficult to love the one who is unlovely and detests the Christian's concern. However, regardless of the difficulty involved, God tells Christians to give the same quality of love to the unlovely person as he gives to himself.

James calls this the royal law. The royal law is first found in Leviticus 19:18 and it is restated in Matthew 22:39 by Christ. It is to be practiced by Christians who are a royal priesthood according to 1 Peter 2:9. Just think of it! When Christians practice this royal law, they are actually having a part in completing the love of God in the world.

VERSE 9

The alternate manner of treating people is given in verse 9. Simply stated it is committing the sin of respect of persons, giving preferential treatment to those who may be able to do something in return while shunning those who cannot.

It is significant to note that James is not talking about the individual who may have committed the sin of respect of persons once or twice. He knows no one is perfect. Instead, he is speaking about the person who habitually shuns others, plays favorites and isolates himself with a select clique.

Degree of Sin

In effect James is saying that while most Christians will not commit major crimes, it is very easy for them to fall prey to sins which they consider to be of less intensity, sins that do not harm others physically, such as the sin of respect of persons. The mark which God has set for every Christian in life is that he may be an effective witness. While the believer may not consider the sin of respect of persons as evil as other sins, it often drives people away from Christ.

James goes on to point out that the habitual sin of partiality puts the believer in the position of being a transgressor of the law. A transgressor may be defined as one who steps out of line, one who deviates from a well-defined course of action. That well-defined course of action as far as the Christian is concerned is that which has been outlined in the Scriptures. When Christians commit the sin of respect of persons, they step out of line. They deviate from the path that God would have them travel. They disappoint the One who redeemed them and bring shame to His name.

VERSES 10, 11

One of the common practices today is that of categorizing sins. The scale is set up in such a way that the worst possible sin is murder and next to it is adultery followed by stealing and lying. James says God does not view sin in this way. Sin in God's eyes is sin. The individual who breaks one of His laws is guilty of breaking the whole law. He stands before God as a lawbreaker.

No believer has a right to consider himself more holy than someone else because his sins are not as bad as that of someone else.

VERSE 12
Speak and Do

There are two commands to consider in this verse. The command to *so speak* demands that the words that pour forth from the Christian's lips be saturated with love. Such words will be free from harshness, from adverse criticism, from bitterness, from egocentric statements and from malicious gossip. They will be words of comfort, concern and compassion.

The command to *so do* (KJV) demands that the activity of the Christian be motivated by love. These two commands taken together indicate that God expects the believer to back up what he says by that which he does—keeping in mind that both his works and actions will be judged in the light of the royal law of love.

VERSE 13

The Christian is going to have to give an account of both his words and his actions when he appears before the judgment seat of Christ. If he has been harsh and critical in his dealings with others, ignoring the royal law of love by showing them no mercy, then he can expect Christ to judge him on the same basis. He will be saved all right, because of the atoning work of Jesus Christ. His rewards, however, will be greatly limited.

James tells the other side of the story at the end of verse 13. The Christian who lives by the royal law of love, does not commit the sin of favoritism and deals with his fellowman in a merciful way can look forward with joyful anticipation to the judgment seat of Christ. The Lord will temper justice with mercy, and great will be the Christian's reward.

FOR REFLECTION

How is the sin of respect of persons practiced in the church where you are attending?

Restate the royal law in your own words.

Footnotes
1. *The Letters of James and Peter,* translated and interpreted by William Barclay. Published by the Saint Andrew Press, Edinburgh, 1958; and in the U.S.A. by the Westminster Press, 1961, p. 73.
2. Barclay, *The Letters of James and Peter,* p. 78.

CHAPTER SIX

THE PERFECT COMBINATION

JAMES 2:14-26

JAMES 2:14-26

14. What use is it, my brethren, if a man says he has faith, but he has no works? Can that faith save him?

15. If a brother or sister is without clothing and in need of daily food,

16. and one of you says to them. "Go in peace, be warmed and be filled", and yet you do not give them what is necessary for *their* body, what use is that?

17. Even so faith, if it has no works, is dead, *being* by itself.

18. But someone may *well* say, "You have faith, and I have works; show me your faith without the works, and I will show you my faith by my works."

19. You believe that God is one. You do well; the demons also believe, and shudder.

20. But are you willing to recognize, you foolish fellow, that faith without works is useless?

21. Was not Abraham our father justified by works, when he offered up Isaac his son on the altar?

22. You see that faith was working with his works, and as a result of the works, faith was perfected;

23. and the Scripture was fulfilled which says, "And Abraham believed God, and it was reckoned to him as righteousness." and he was called the friend of God.

24. You see that a man is justified by works, and not by faith alone.
25. And in the same way was not Rahab the harlot also justified by works, when she received the messengers and sent them out by another way?
26. For just as the body without *the* spirit is dead, so also faith without works is dead.

Christianity, contrary to what a great number of professing Christians believe, is not just faith or works. It is both faith and works.

A cold, austere, intellectual faith, void of action is nothing more than a mental assent to the existence of God. This faith is just one step above atheism. It is long on profession but short on practice, prolific in words but poverty-stricken in works. It is hypocrisy raised to the superlative degree.

James teaches that this cold, intellectual type of faith is dead. The person who says he is a Christian but gives no evidence of it by what he does is James' target. This person joins the church but refuses to serve, give or even attend unless it is convenient.

VERSES 14,15 16

James tells the story of a professing Christian who says he has faith. Notice that the man says he has faith, James doesn't say it. This person has a brother come to him in need of food and clothing. Instead of providing these for him, or at least working out a plan whereby the man himself could provide them, this so-called Christian says to him, "I am so sorry about your condition.

Vital faith, the faith that marks the difference between heaven and hell, always manifests itself in righteous deeds.

You go on your way and I will pray for you. I trust that you will find enough food and proper clothing. Peace be to you, my brother."

VERSES 17, 18

This type of faith is worthless. It is dead. Such an attitude on the part of this professing Christian is positive proof that he is spiritually dead. He is nothing but a hypocrite.

Interwoven throughout this chapter is a great and important truth, namely that vital faith, the faith that marks the difference between heaven and hell, always manifests itself in righteous deeds.

James, using the spiritual imagination with which God had endowed him, pictures two men, both of whom ostensibly are Christians. They stand in contrast one to the other because of the completely antithetical means that they employ in making known their professed Christianity. Both of these men have many modern counterparts.

Words

The first man is one who stands and tells you, "I believe in Jesus Christ as my Savior, therefore I am a Christian." On the surface this testimony sounds good. However, don't be too hasty with this conclusion. This man may succeed in convincing himself that once he has made this verbal declaration, he has no further responsibility. He can live as he pleases, disregard God's moral law whenever it suits his convenience and indulge the flesh to the full without any compunction of conscience whatsoever.

There is a widespread movement within protestant-ism today that takes the position that one's willingness to declare verbally his faith in Christ is all that is necessary to make him a Christian. Those who are in the vanguard of this movement argue that our world being what it is makes it impossible for a person to live according to the teachings of God's Word. They contend that the moral standards of the Bible must be lowered in order for the Christian to be compatible with his non-Christian contemporaries.

Deeds

The second man is one who declares his faith in Christ as Savior and then substantiates that declaration with righteous deeds. The faith that marks the difference between heaven and hell in the life of a person, always manifests itself in righteous deeds.

The manuscript for *Markings* by Dag Hammarskjold was found with a note pinned to it which said, "A sort of white book concerning my negotiations with myself and with my God." In the book, Hammarskjold makes an observation which is a good description of the thinking of this second man that James presents. "In our time the road to holiness necessarily leads into and through the field of action."

VERSE 19

The individual who claims belief in God but whose faith is dead does not really have anything. Even the devils themselves believe that God exists. There is no virtue in this.

VERSE 20

James characterizes the faith of the person who does not help his brother as foolish. This is translated from the Greek word *kene* which means *empty*. Linguistic scholar R.C. Trench comments, "When used not of things but of persons, *kenos* predicates not merely an absence and emptiness of good, but, since the moral nature of man endures no vacuum, the presence of the contrary."[1]

VERSE 21
Abraham

James is so eager for people to understand this truth that he illustrates it. First he calls attention to Abraham. He points out that this revered patriarch demonstrated his faith in God by perfect obedience. When God instructed him to offer Isaac as a sacrifice, Abraham, though heartbroken, did exactly as he was told to do. Just before he made the sacrifice, God stayed his hand and provided a ram as a substitute (see Gen. 22:1-13). This is a picture of the substitutionary death of the Lord Jesus Christ in behalf of every believer.

VERSES 22, 23

Because of his act of obedience, three things happened. When Abraham placed his faith in God, immediately the righteousness of God was given to him whereby all of his sins were forgiven and he became a part of God's family. This is exactly what happens when an individual commits himself in faith to Jesus Christ. The very righteousness of Jesus Christ is given to him.

His sins are forgiven, and he is made a member of God's eternal family and citizen of His everlasting kingdom.

VERSE 24

Because of his perfect faith and obedience, Abraham stood before God justified. He showed a total reliance on God. Abraham was a genuine believer who demonstrated his faith by his action. In Philippians 2:12, Paul agrees with James and says in essence, "Through faith God has bestowed upon you the gift of salvation. You have it within you. God knows that you have it, and you know that you have it. Now it is your responsibility to work it out, that is, to demonstrate that you possess it by righteous deeds. In this way your friends and neighbors will know that you have it."

VERSE 25
Rahab

James also recalls the story of Rahab who sheltered God's servants doing reconnaissance work in Jericho. She proved by her works that she was a woman of faith. She was rewarded with her life and the lives of her family (see Josh. 6:25).

Christians must do just as Abraham and Rahab did in demonstrating a saving faith by conforming to God's will in their lives.

Two gentlemen were crossing the river in a rowboat when they got into an argument about faith and works. The man rowing turned to them and said, "I believe I can resolve your argument. In my hands I have two oars which I call faith and works. If I pull on one without the other, all we do is go around in circles. If I pull on both of them simultaneously, we move forward toward our destination. This is the way it is with faith and works. Faith without works will not suffice. Neither will works without faith. We make progress toward our destination when we allow the two to work together in our lives."

VERSE 26

James now completes his discussion of cold intellectual faith. What a graphic picture this is! When physical death occurs, the soul is separated from the body. Immediately the body begins to decay and decompose. For people's protection it must be buried soon. James says the person who intellectually assents to the doctrines of Christianity without practicing them is spiritually like a dead body. Decay will ultimately separate him eternally from God and Christian loved ones. His only hope is to repent, commit himself completely to Jesus Christ and begin to demonstrate his faith by his actions.

FOR REFLECTION

What is the difference between a dead faith and a vital faith?

Using Abraham and Rahab as examples, what happens to the person who commits his life in faith to God?

Footnote
1. R.C. Trench, *Synonyms of the New Testament* (Grand Rapids: Wm. B. Eerdmans Publishing Co., 1950).

CHAPTER SEVEN

SMALL BUT POWERFUL

JAMES 3:1-12

JAMES 3:1-12

1. Let not many *of you* become teachers, my brethren, knowing that as such we shall incur a stricter judgment.
2. For we all stumble in many *ways*. If any one does not stumble in what he says, he is a perfect man, able to bridle the whole body as well.
3. Now if we put the bits into the horses' mouths so that they may obey us, we direct their entire body as well.
4. Behold, the ships also, though they are so great and are driven by strong winds, are still directed by a very small rudder, wherever the inclination of the pilot desires.
5. So also the tongue is a small part of the body, and *yet* it boasts of great things. Behold, how great a forest is set aflame by such a small fire!
6. And the tongue is a fire, the *very* world of iniquity; the tongue is set among our members as that which defiles the entire body, and sets on fire the course of *our* life, and is set on fire by hell.
7. For every species of beasts and birds, of reptiles and creatures of the sea, is tamed, and has been tamed by the human race.
8. But no one can tame the tongue; *it is* a restless evil *and* full of deadly poison.
9. With it we bless *our* Lord and Father; and with it we curse men, who have been made in the likeness of God;

10. from the same mouth come *both* blessing and cursing. My brethren, these things ought not to be this way.
11. Does a fountain send out from the same opening *both* fresh and bitter *water*?
12. Can a fig tree, my brethren, produce olives, or a vine produce figs? Neither *can* salt water produce fresh.

It is rather significant that James introduces the subject of the tongue at this point in his Epistle. Up to now his emphasis has been upon works, not words. Unmercifully he castigated those who with their lips professed faith but with their lives denied it. Now in this passage, he summarizes the biblical teaching concerning the use of the tongue.

All of James' comments are as applicable today as the day he wrote them. These first 12 verses of chapter 3, perhaps more than all of the others, need to be emphasized in evangelical churches. Legion is the number of those whose names are on the rolls of Bible-preaching and Bible-believing churches who would not think of committing the more heinous sins of murder, stealing, adultery or drunkenness. But they do not hesitate to assassinate with their tongues the character of their fellow Christians.

Someone has said that great minds discuss ideas, average minds discuss events and small minds discuss people. If this is an accurate criterion, there are a great many evangelical Christians in this third category. What the world needs is churches filled with people who practice the teaching of James 3:1-12. If the time ever comes when this happens, many of our present-day problems will disappear. The place where we need to begin implementing the teaching of this passage is in refusing to listen to church members who speak in a derogatory manner about other believers.

VERSE 1
Rabbis/Teachers

In Judaism, of which Christianity is the true fulfillment, the most respected person was the religious teacher. He was called *rabbi,* which actually means, "My great one." Everywhere he went he was accorded the utmost respect. The Jewish people believed that a man's duty to his rabbi exceeded his duty to his parents because his parents were able to provide for him only physical life while through the rabbi he received spiritual life. It was actually stated that if a man's parents and his rabbi were captured by an enemy, it was the man's duty to ransom the rabbi first. If both were in need of physical provisions, it was his responsibility to give the rabbi preferential treatment.

Even a cursory study of Judaism reveals that there were many great and dedicated rabbis. But many men went into the profession primarily because they loved the plaudits and praise of the crowd. When the New Testament church came into being, this sense of respect and place of honor accorded the rabbis was transferred by the early Hebrew converts to the teachers of Christianity. Unfortunately in the early church, just as in Judaism, there were those who set themselves up as teachers because they wanted the acclaim of their fellow believers. As the result of this false motivation, there were teachers who did not live according to that which they taught (see Rom. 2:17-19), teachers who

taught before they knew anything themselves (see 1
Tim. 1:6,7) and false teachers who cared nothing for
sound doctrine but taught what they thought the people
wanted to hear (see 2 Tim. 4:3).

A Warning

James actually warns against anyone becoming a
teacher for selfish reasons such as that of desiring position, prominence and the plaudits of the crowd. Today
this advice is appropriate for pastors, evangelists, pro-
fessors, denominational workers and Sunday School
teachers. All those who have direct responsibility for
teaching by word of mouth the basic truth of the Scriptures must be sure that they are called of God to this
position.

In order to be effective in this place of high calling,
the Christian teacher/leader must be willing to pay the
price of a deep, daily devotional life, the price of hours
of study under the leadership of the Holy Spirit, the price
of having a teachable spirit whereby he can learn from
others and the price of substantiating his teaching by
the way he lives.

James does not stop here. He goes on to point out
the reason why the teacher should measure up to this
high standard. The teacher, and James includes himself
in this statement with the word *we*, will be judged more
strictly. James is saying that when Christians appear
before the judgment seat of Christ, teachers will be separated from their brethren and judged by a much higher
standard than the others. They will be judged on the
basis of what they taught, what they spoke in the name
of Christ and what they articulated with their tongues.

Just because the standard for Christian teachers is a

high one, this is no reason for Christians to shirk responsibility by saying, "I can never meet the requirements,
therefore, I won't teach." If God has called a person, He
is going to hold that person responsible for yielding to
that call. The person who refuses is outside of God's will
for his life, a very unenviable position in which to be.

To the extent a believer is able to control his tongue,
to that extent and only to that extent is he mature in the
faith. The moment one who claims to be a Christian
loses his temper or utters one word of gossip about
another person, at that moment he shows himself a
spiritual baby. This is true regardless of the physical age
of the individual involved.

VERSE 2
Tongue Control

All people have a problem in this matter of keeping the
tongue under control. James is honest in including himself in the indictment that all slip up in many ways as far
as tongue control is concerned. Sometimes that slip-up
may be in the form of an off-color story or profanity due
to anger. Sometimes it expresses itself in idle gossip
and at other times in a dishonest statement or a half-
truth.

The stalwarts of the faith, the patriarchs of the ages
had feet of clay when it came to controlling their
tongues. Moses "spoke rashly with his lips" (Ps. 106:33),
and Peter had his problems at this point (see Mark 14:71).
After the Lord told the disciples that all of them would
be offended because of Him that very night, the night of
His betrayal and arrest, Peter spoke up and in effect
said, "Lord, these other disciples may have a problem
when danger arises, but not me. I am Simon Peter, the

Rock. You can count on me to remain faithful to you even if it costs me my life." Jesus looked at Peter with eyes of pity. "'Peter,' Jesus said, 'before the cock crows a second time tomorrow morning you will deny me three times'" (Mark 14:30, *TLB.*). In spite of his protestations over this pronouncement, in just a few hours Simon sinned with his tongue as he denied the Savior three times, cursing and uttering oaths to back up his denials (see Mark 14:66-72).

Every child of God has a problem that centers around the words that fall from his lips. This includes the great, the near-great and the not-so-great. The true sign of Christian maturity is the ability of the Christian to control his tongue.

There are two interesting words in the second half of verse 2. The first word is translated *perfect* from the Greek word *teleios*. It means perfect—not in the sense of sinless perfection—in the sense of completeness and maturity. The second word is translated *bridle* from the Greek word *kalinagagasi*. It is used in the sense of an excellent horseman bridling a good horse. The expert horseman knows when to rein in his horse, bringing him to a complete stop. Just so, a mature Christian knows how to control a conversation so that he can listen while others speak. He also knows when to release the reins and let the horse go. He knows when to speak so as both to inform and inspire those to whom he is speaking.

God needs men and women who, led by the Holy Spirit, know what to say in order to bolster the faith and strengthen the courage of their faltering Christian brothers and sisters. Such Christians are truly mature in the faith.

Mastery over the tongue is a struggle. The devil sees

to that. He does not quit tempting Christians. He may momentarily withdraw while seeking new and more sinister ways of attacking. There are several things which can be done in order to win this battle and achieve Christian maturity.

Ways of Control

Scripture teaches the use of all the willpower available in order to defeat the enemy. This was one of King David's methods which he declares in Psalm 39:1.

Another way is to pray daily for divine help in defeating the enemy. Jesus supports this in John 16:23.

When a person surrenders totally to the control of the Holy Spirit, he receives from the Holy Spirit the ability to control the tongue. It is impossible for Satan to gain the victory.

Do not be frustrated by a setback, for frustration only leads to one defeat after another. Frustration and defeat are problems most Christians have. There are those who finally come to the place where they reason something like this, "It is impossible for me to control my tongue. I am not alone in this. No one else is able to do it either. Every person is fallible. I, therefore, am no longer going to try. I'll say what I want to, in the way I want to and whenever I want to. I am not going to concern myself about it anymore."

There is a commonly known story that comes from the life of Martin Luther that is germane to this type of rationalization. It is said that the devil approached him one day and tried to use the fact that every person is fallible. He presented the reformer with a long list of sins of which he was guilty. When he had finished Luther said to him, "Think a little harder; you must have forgotten some." This the devil did and added other sins to the list. At the conclusion of this, Martin Luther simply said, "That's fine. Now write across that list in red ink, 'The blood of Jesus Christ, His Son, cleanseth us from all sin.'" There was nothing the devil could say to that.

Instead of developing a defeatist attitude over failures, Christians should realize that Christ is ready, willing and able to forgive even the sins of the misuse of the tongue. Instead of frustration, there should be confession. First John 1:9 makes this clear.

The Christian who is honestly concerned enough to fight for tongue control will ask for God's help and surrender unequivocally and without reservation to the control of the Holy Spirit. When he falters, he will confess it and receive forgiveness. He will come to the place where he can bridle his tongue and will thereby become more mature in the faith.

There is only one person who ever lived who never made a slip of the tongue. That person is the Lord Jesus Christ.

VERSE 3

After giving special instructions to teachers concerning the use of the tongue in verse 1 and after pointing out that the control of the tongue is a sign of Christian maturity in verse 2, James answered a question which he realized would be in the minds of the discerning readers of this Epistle.

Importance of Size

Imagine, just for a moment, a conversation with James which would go something like this. "James, you know

No man can tame the
tongue. What man
cannot do, God can do.

that from the standpoint of size, the tongue is one of the most insignificant parts of the body. It is not nearly as large as the foot, the ankle, the knee, the hand or the head. Could something so small be as important as you say—even to the point of indicating how mature a Christian is in his faith? This is incredible!"

James answers this question by using two illustrations that are familiar to nearly everyone both then and now. The first illustration is that of a bit in the mouth of a horse. From the standpoint of size, it is a very inconsequential piece of equipment, and yet it is of paramount importance to a horseman for it is the means by which he controls his mount. This small piece of iron, bent in the right way and connected to the bridle in a proper manner, is so important to the equestrian that it can actually mean the difference between life or death to him.

VERSE 4

The second illustration which James uses is that of the rudder of a ship. Years before James was born, the Greek philosopher Aristotle used this same picture in writing about the science of mechanics. He said that a rudder is small and attached to the very end of the ship. But it has so much power that one man with this little rudder can move the great bulk of a ship.

What the bit is to the horse and the rudder is to the oceangoing liner, the tongue is to the personality and character of the Christian. If the Christian allows the Holy Spirit to use his tongue as the expert horseman uses the bit and the captain of a ship the rudder, his life will conform completely to the will of God. He will be an effective servant, and his witness will bear fruit.

The basic life principle in these illustrations is that those things which outwardly seem small, insignificant and inconsequential can often be of great importance. In God's sight each person is of infinite value. Even though a person may consider himself insignificant in the eyes of his contemporaries, he is not in God's sight. So valuable is he to God that even the hairs of his head are numbered (see Matt. 10:30). He is worth more to God than all the wealth in the world.

VERSES 5, 6
Potential for Evil

James calls attention to the fourfold evil potential of the tongue. Though small, the tongue is one of the most active members of the body. It can be destructive, deceptive, dangerous and hypocritical.

The tongue carelessly used is analogous in its destructive power to a small flame that is mishandled. Such a flame can turn the loveliest forest into a holocaust of destruction. Experience teaches that even a well-intentioned, mature Christian who gets careless and doesn't think before he speaks can be destructive in what he says.

VERSES 7, 8

Even though man has successfully tamed almost every living creature—the birds, the serpents and the fish—he has not yet come to the place where he can completely control his tongue. Just the time he thinks he has this situation well in hand, he will slip and say something he later regrets. Each person has had the experience of making a statement at one time or another which he has lived to regret. Notice something subtle about this deceptive potential of the tongue. James does not say that the tongue cannot be tamed. He does say that no man can tame the tongue. What man cannot do, God can do. The individual who will daily yield his tongue to the control of the Holy Spirit can overcome this deceptive potential.

One of the most dangerous potential uses of the tongue is gossip. Gossip can strike far and no matter how much sincere effort is put forth, its evil effects cannot be completely overcome.

A little girl came to her mother early one morning and asked, "Mommie, which is worse, to tell a lie or to steal?" The mother assured her that both were equally bad. The child's response startled the mother. She said, "Well, I think lying is worse than stealing." When the mother asked why, she explained, "If you steal a thing, you can take it back or pay for it. But a lie is forever."

VERSES 9, 10

The tongue can be the most hypocritical thing in the world. At times it is used to bless God and other times it is used to curse men. A man comes to church on Sunday and sings the praises of his Savior, and then on Monday he gets mad at one of his contemporaries and curses him out.

VERSES 11, 12

Three illustrations point out the absolute absurdity of such hypocrisy. Just as it is impossible for a fountain to produce both salt and fresh water at the same time, just as it is impossible for a fig tree to bear olives and just as it is impossible for a grapevine to bear figs—so it should be impossible for a believer to say anything that would harm the cause of the Savior. Those who claim to love the Lord should both seek and take advantage of opportunities to extol the virtues of the Savior.

The main speaker at a convention was Alvin Dark, former manager of the San Francisco Giants. After spending the first 10 minutes talking about baseball, Mr. Dark said something like this. "Before I conclude my talk, I want to tell you about the most important thing in all the world to me, my own personal faith in Jesus Christ as Savior and Lord. When I was a boy growing up in Lake Charles, Louisiana, the day came when I realized that I was a lost sinner. As I listened to my pastor and studied my Bible I discovered that God loved me so much that He sent His only begotten Son, the Lord Jesus Christ, to die on Calvary and then to arise from the dead three days later. As a lad I trusted this same Jesus as my Savior and my Lord. I have never regretted this decision. It is the most important one I ever made."

This, my friend, is the proper use of the tongue.

FOR REFLECTION

Why is the teacher judged by a higher standard?

What are the ways a Christian can work toward control of the tongue?

Listen carefully to what you say in the next 24 hours. Is your tongue a blessing to God and man?

CHAPTER EIGHT

THE WALK OF WISDOM

JAMES 3:13-18

13. Who among you is wise and understanding? Let him show by his good behavior his deeds in the gentleness of wisdom.
14. But if you have bitter jealousy and selfish ambition in your heart, do not be arrogant and *so* lie against the truth.
15. This wisdom is not that which comes down from above, but is earthly, natural, demonic.
16. For where jealousy and selfish ambition exist, there is disorder and every evil thing.
17. But the wisdom from above is first pure, then peaceable, gentle, reasonable, full of mercy and good fruits, unwavering, without hypocrisy.
18. And the seed whose fruit is righteousness is sown in peace by those who make peace.

VERSES 13—16

James introduces the second section of the third chapter with a thought-provoking, spiritually and intellectually stimulating question. In answering the question, he calls attention to two types of wisdom available to every individual.

There is that type of wisdom that is earthly, sensual and devilish. It takes no account of God whatsoever. It approaches life as if the Almighty did not exist. It results in bitter envying, strife, confusion and every evil work.

Tragically, this is the type of wisdom that in reality is pseudowisdom, which the majority of the people throughout the world are buying today. This is the reason that every daily newspaper every day of the week is filled with stories of international conflict, murder, stealing, divorce and every other crime the mind can conceive.

Then there is that type of wisdom which comes from God. This wisdom He is anxious and eager to bestow upon all who will receive it in faith. It has seven distinguishing characteristics which James delineates.

VERSES 17, 18
Pure

The first of these characteristics is purity. The use of the word *first* in this verse is most significant. It implies that if a person is not pure, he will not have any of the other characteristics of true wisdom.If a person is pure in the inner recesses of his being, then he will be in a position to acquire the other six characteristics of wisdom. If he is not, he doesn't have a chance of acquiring them. Because of God's mercy and grace toward man, this characteristic can be a reality in the experience of everyone who is willing in faith to invite Jesus Christ into his heart to become the Savior and Master of his life.

Peaceable

God's wisdom is first pure, then peaceable. There is a natural and beautiful connection between these two. The Bible teaches that the individual who has been made pure through his faith in Jesus Christ as Lord and

Savior has established peace between himself and God. Once an individual has established this peace on a vertical level between himself and his Maker, he will then do his best to have a peaceable relationship with his fellowman on a horizontal level.

In the teachings of the Lord Jesus Christ, this same natural sequence of a right vertical relationship resulting in a correct horizontal relationship is emphasized. When answering the lawyer employed by the Pharisees, Jesus did not limit Himself to one commandment. He gave two in Matthew 22:37-39. The person who truly loves God with all of his heart, soul and mind will have a natural desire to love his neighbor as himself. A right vertical relationship always motivates the individual to desire a correct horizontal relationship. This is true as far as both love and peace are concerned.

The story is told of a young minister who was going home late one Sunday evening from church. As he entered the streetcar with his Bible under his arm, he immediately became the target of some insulting and sneering remarks from several rough characters. As the preacher started to disembark, one of the gang laughingly said, "Mister, how far is it to heaven?" Quietly and with dignity the young minister said, "It is only a step. Will you take it now?" This reply plus the peaceable attitude the preacher had toward his tormentors resulted later in his questioner coming to know Christ as Savior.

Gentle

The word translated *gentle* comes from the Greek word, *epieikes*. Scholars are agreed that this is one of the most difficult, if not *the* most difficult words in the Greek language to translate.

Aristotle defined its meaning when he wrote that it is *epieikes* to pardon human failings, to look to lawyers and not to the law, to look at the intention and not the action, to remember good rather than evil, to see the good one has received rather than the good one has done, to put up with injurious treatment, to wish to settle a matter by words rather than deeds and lastly, to prefer arbitration to judgment.

This word *epieikes* conveys the idea of tempering justice with mercy. Take for example the landlord who owns a number of apartments. One of these is occupied by a hard-working widow with four small children. For months she faithfully pays the rent. Then one day she becomes so ill she is unable to work. Her income is cut off. The landlord knows that strict legality is on his side. He can force her to move if he so desires. However, as he looks at this woman and understands her plight, he has empathy for her. He realizes that the circumstances confronting her are beyond her control. Instead of throwing her out in the street, he allows her to remain in the apartment. In addition, he helps her to work out her problems of providing the necessities of life for herself and her children. He tempers justice with mercy.

Epieikes conveys the idea of being willing to go the second mile, of being always willing to forgive regardless of the circumstances and of extending kindness to one's enemies.

Jesus Christ is the only person who ever personified *epieikes* perfectly. This He did at Calvary. On the cross He tempered justice with mercy. Justice demanded death and hell for every man. Through His sacrifice the Lord met the demands of justice and provided the gift of eternal redemption for all who are willing to accept it in

True wisdom, godly wisdom, is characterized by mercy which expresses itself in Christlike activity in behalf of others.

faith. It was on the cross that Jesus went the second mile in order to establish peace between God and man. He made forgiveness, God's divine forgiveness, available to man. Jesus showed kindness for His enemies as He prayed, "Father, forgive them; for they do not know what they are doing" (Luke 23:34).

Reasonable

This characteristic of wisdom has inherent within it the idea of obedience and the idea of being willing to listen to reason. Absolute obedience to the will of God is a must in order to be counted wise in His sight. Involved in this willingness is a determination to acknowledge Jesus Christ not only as Savior but also as Lord.

It is at this point that most people who call themselves Christians fall. They are willing for Jesus Christ to be their Savior by providing for them that which they cannot provide for themselves. The matter of acknowledging His Lordship, however, is quite a different story. Sometimes it isn't convenient to comply with His directives. Christ prayed, "Not My will, but Thine be done" (Luke 22:42). Those in defiance of the One who loved so much that He died for these same people act as if they were praying, "Not Thy will but *mine* be done."

There is an interesting anecdote which fits at this point. It has to do with a university student who went to hear a gifted speaker lecture on the first chapter of Genesis. Throughout the evening the speaker played on two words: *let* and *God*. When the young man went home that night these words were ringing in his ears, "Let God! Let God! Let God!" So impressed was he by these words that he carved them out in wooden letters and hung them in his room.

For the next few days he thought constantly about them. Let God! But how could he let God? In desperation one morning he banged the door of his room with his fist, saying, "How can I let God have control of my life? It is impossible!"

When he came home that night, he discovered to his utter amazement that when he had struck the door of his room that morning, the letter *d* had fallen off the word *God*. His sign now read, "Let Go." He had the answer for which he was searching. He had to let go of the things in his life which he knew were contrary to God's will in order that God might have complete control of him. From then on the motto of his life was, "Let go and let God." This is exactly what the wise person must do. He must let go of his life and let God the Holy Spirit have complete control. This is the absolute obedience demanded of the Christian.

The man who is wise in God's sight is willing to listen to reason. He isn't so conceited as to believe that he has the answer to every question and the solution to each problem. This does not imply that he is either a weakling or a compromiser. Instead, it means that when any difficulty arises, he is willing to prayerfully look at it from every standpoint before he decides on his course of action.

Unfortunately, this characteristic is absent in the lives of many people who claim to love Jesus Christ. These individuals are willful, stubborn, egotistical and unbending. They are modern pharisees, demanding that everyone cross his *t*'s and dot his *i*'s exactly as they do. Convinced that they have the last word on everything, they are willing to trample underfoot anyone who disagrees with them. They do irreparable damage to the cause of Christ and seemingly take a fiendish delight in so doing.

Full of Mercy and Good Fruits

The man who is truly wise is one who is filled to over-flowing with mercy for others; mercy which issues in good fruits; mercy which motivates him to care for those less fortunate than he. This is mercy showing itself as practical help. Christian pity is not merely an emotion. Christian pity is action. It is action motivated by mercy.

It is easy to feel sorry for someone who has fallen on hard times through no fault of his own. It is commend-able to be quick and ready to help this person. How-ever, to be truly wise in God's sight the Christian must be just as quick and ready to help someone who is in diffi-culty because of what he has willfully done. This type of mercy is but a dim reflection of the mercy of Almighty God which was manifest at Calvary. True wisdom, godly wisdom, is characterized by mercy which expresses itself in Christlike activity in behalf of others.

Unwavering, Without Hypocrisy

A wise man in God's sight does not push himself for-ward as some great and distinguished personality. He realizes that like any other Christian, he is nothing more than a sinner saved by grace and, therefore, a servant of the Lord Jesus Christ. He is one who at all times is will-ing to humble himself before the Lord.

The story is told that one Sunday morning while the Duke of Wellington was kneeling at the altar of the par-ish church to receive the elements of the Lord's Supper, a very poor, old man came up and knelt close by him. Someone touched the poor man on the shoulder and suggested to him that he should either move farther away from the Duke or get up and wait for this great man of state to be served.

The Duke, sensing what was happening, clasped the old man's hand and in a distinct and reverential tone he said, "Do not move. We are all equal here."

The true meaning of being without hypocrisy is found in studying the history of the theatre. In the ancient Greek plays, the actors were called hypocrites. On the stage they professed to be something they weren't. Unfortunately, there are many people who go through life playacting. They profess to be something they are not. They are hypocrites. They fool no one with this false veneer, this facade, this hypocrisy, except themselves. What they really are is well-known to God and their acquaintances with the result that they are displeasing to both.

Hypocrites are like the bat in one of Aesop's fables that tells of the war between the birds and the beasts. This particular bat was an opportunist. He tried to be on both sides. When the birds were victorious, he would fly around claiming that he was one of them. When the beasts prevailed, he would walk around stating that he was a beast. It wasn't long until both repudiated him and he had to hide himself. This, according to Aesop, is the reason that the bat now appears only at night.[1]

The hypocritical, playacting Christian, the one whose faith is mere profession, will eventually drive people away from the Lord Jesus Christ. Through the years innumerable people have gone to a Christless grave to spend eternity in hell because of the hypocrisy of many who call themselves Christians.

It is said that Thomas K. Beecher could not stand deceit of any kind. When he discovered that the clock in his church ran habitually either too slow or too fast, he reportedly put a placard on the wall above it that read in large letters, "Don't blame my hands—the trouble lies deeper." Don't make the mistake of promising to be a better Christian. The trouble is not on the outside; it is in the inner recesses of a person's being. Only Christ can cure this malady. This He will do if a person in genuine repentance seeks His forgiveness and turns himself over to Him in simple childlike faith.

FOR REFLECTION

List the characteristics of wisdom. Explain why purity is the first one.

What is the historical meaning of the word hypocrisy?

What contemporary word or words would you use today?

Footnote
1. Spiros Zodhiates, *The Work of Faith* (Grand Rapids: Wm. B. Eerdmans Publishing Co.). Used by permission.

CHAPTER NINE

THE CAUSE AND CURE FOR TROUBLE

JAMES 4:1-6

JAMES 4:1-6

1. What is the source of quarrels and conflicts among you? Is not the source your pleasures that wage war in your members?
2. You lust and do not have; *so* you commit murder. And you are envious and cannot obtain; *so* you fight and quarrel. You do not have because you do not ask.
3. You ask and do not receive, because you ask with wrong motives, so that you may spend *it* on your pleasures.
4. You adulteresses, do you not know that friendship with the world is hostility toward God? Therefore whoever wishes to be a friend of the world makes himself an enemy of God.
5. Or do you think that the Scripture speaks to no purpose: "He jealously desires the spirit which He has made to dwell in us"?
6. But He gives a greater grace. Therefore *it* says, "God is opposed to the proud, but gives grace to the humble."

VERSE 1

Gripping, informative and challenging words open the fourth chapter of the Epistle. The central truth of these words is that the uncontrolled passions and desires in the hearts of individuals are the source of every evil act that has ever taken place.

One New Testament scholar has pointed out that the steps in the process of an evil deed becoming a reality are easy to trace. "A man allows himself to desire something. That thing begins to dominate his thoughts. He finds himself involuntarily thinking about it in his waking hours and dreaming of it when he sleeps. It begins to be what is aptly called a ruling passion. He then begins to form imaginary plans and schemes of how he may obtain it. These plans and schemes may well involve imaginary ways of eliminating those who stand in his way. But then one day the imaginings may blaze into action and he may find himself taking the necessary and terrible steps to obtain his desire."[1]

Many of the great philosophers believed and taught this same truth. Plato explained it like this: "The sole cause of wars and revolutions and battles is nothing other than the body and its desires."[2] The great Roman orator, Cicero, had this to say: "It is unsatiable desires which overturn not only individual men, but whole families, and which even bring down the state. From desires there spring hatred, schisms, discords, seditions and wars."[3]

James begins with a significant question in verse 1 of chapter 4, a question that is accurately suggestive of that which is taking place on far too many fronts within Christendom. In effect James is saying, "Tell me, Christians, why are so many of you hostile and contentious in your attitude toward each other even to the point of dividing your churches?" And the implication of the question is, "Don't you know that this contention and cantankerous spirit damages the cause of Christ?"

The first century churches had their difficulties too. The New Testament makes this clear in the sixth chapter of Acts. The Greek members of the church were really upset because they felt that as far as the welfare funds were concerned their widows were coming off second-best to the Hebrew widows. So sharp was the division resulting from this that the first board of deacons any church ever had was elected to care for this matter.

The Corinthian church had a fight over preachers. In the book of Philippians a fight occurred in the "Ladies' Missionary Society" of that church. There was a bitter and raging struggle in practically every New Testament church over whether or not a Christian must first adhere to the ceremonial laws of the Jews.

After raising this question as to why Christians so many times have a hostile and contentious spirit, James answers with another question. The contention and hostility so often seen among Christians resulting in dissension and division in the churches is due to the fight that is constantly going on in the life of every believer. This fight is between the carnal nature of the Christian, his evil desires, passions and desire for pleasure, and the Spirit of God who dwells within him.

Mark this well and never forget it! When an individual becomes a Christian, all of his troubles are not over. The devil will see to that. With all of his diabolical power, he will fiendishly stimulate evil passions and desires to the point that if a person is not both careful and determined, he will find himself constantly turning his back upon the leadership of the Holy Spirit.

Even the greatest Christians have had and do have a problem with this internal struggle. A case in point is the apostle Paul. No one who ever lived was more dedicated to Christ than this productive and constructive missionary to the Gentiles. And yet he was constantly vexed by the struggle that was going on within him.

VERSES 2, 3
You Lust

Some Christians do succumb to their evil passions and thereby become troublemakers in the church. The first group mentioned is made up of those Christians who are exceedingly ambitious to achieve personal glory. James points out that in every church there are those who want personal glory and the praise of men. They set ambitious goals for themselves. Because their motivation is wrong, they don't make it. The inference is that this failure causes them to be hostile and contentious troublemakers. How right James is! One man set his heart upon becoming a deacon in his church. He felt that this position would give him the prestige and prominence which he greatly desired. When he didn't make it, he became caustic and critical and threatened to leave his church.

Christians must seek the will of the Lord, letting Him set the goals. After finding His will in the matter, they should then proceed to do their respective jobs to the best of their abilities, being careful to give Him all the praise and the glory for whatever accomplishments might result.

You Murder

The next group are those Christians who murder. Obviously James doesn't mean killing people physically. The key to understanding this is found in the meaning of the word *murder* which is translated from the Greek word *phonuete*. It has a metaphorical meaning which is "the killing or the assassination of character or reputation." Unfortunately, in every church there seems to be those who take fiendish delight in assassinating the character, the good name and the impeccable reputation of fellow church members.

A man belonged to an outstanding church for more than 50 years. For some unknown reason he did not like two of the ministers who served that church. He used the same method to try to destroy each man. He employed a detective and instructed him to photograph the pastor in a compromising situation with a secretary. He wanted to use the pictures for blackmail. His plan was thwarted in each case because these ministers were above reproach. Most people would never go to that extreme to try to destroy the good reputation of a fellow church member. However, at times don't they slip just a little with their tongues? Be assured of this, a careless word can be just as devastating as a picture. The lips of the Christian should be used in praising God, not in destroying man.

You Envy

Then there are those troublemakers in the church whose activities are motivated by envy and jealousy. Any Christian who is motivated by envy will inevitably be contentious and hostile in his attitude toward others and a troublemaker wherever he goes.

If ever there was a man whom God raised up for evangelism, that man is Billy Graham. He has spoken to more people about Christ than any other man that ever lived. More people have made public decisions for Christ under his ministry than under the ministry of any other preacher that ever lived. His phenomenal success can be explained in only one way: God. Billy is quick to give the Lord full credit. And, yet, there was a period when hundreds of so-called evangelicals attacked him. A careful analysis of the situation revealed that all the criticism started with two old-time evangelists bitten hard by the green-eyed monster of jealousy. Through their influence this opposition started.

Billy didn't fight back. He just continued to preach, souls continued to be saved and the Lord received the glory and the praise.

You Ask Not

Other hostile, contentious, church troublemakers are those who either neglect their prayer life completely or pervert it. The quickest way to get out of fellowship with the Lord is either by neglecting to pray or by praying for the sole purpose of achieving selfish ends. Real joy, real happiness in the Christian life is derived from close fellowship with the Savior through sincere, unselfish prayer.

During the days of World War II, Chaplain Wyeth Willard conducted a Bible class and prayer meeting on board a ship headed toward Tarawa, an island in the Gilbert Islands' chain. About 15 dedicated Christian boys attended. On the night before they hit the beach, they had a circle of prayer. Every one of the boys prayed something like this: "Lord, tomorrow we are going to storm the beaches of Tarawa. Our officers have told us that this is going to be a bloody battle. Many of our number will be killed. If this has to be, Lord, let us who know Thee be killed and spare those who do not, that they may have more time to make their decision for Thee. In Jesus' name, Amen."

This is high quality, unselfish praying. Those boys could do it because they were close to the Savior. They had neither neglected nor perverted their prayer life.

VERSE 4
Source of Trouble

Notice the strong language James uses in addressing those who are the source of trouble in the church. He is not speaking of physical infidelity but spiritual infidelity. In effect James is saying, "You that constantly are striving for personal glory, you that delight in assassinating the character of your fellow Christian, you that are motivated by envy and you that either neglect your prayer life or pervert it for selfish ends—you are guilty of literally breaking the heart of the One who loved you so much that He went all the way to Calvary to purchase your redemption." One more thing needs to be added here. Not only are the Christians just mentioned guilty of breaking the heart of the Savior, but so is every believer who willfully disobeys the commands of his Lord.

In verse 4 James asks and answers a question. The word *know* is a significant one in this verse. It is translated from the Greek word *oidate* which means "to know by observation and reflection." The implication here is that every Christian should be able to know the devastating effects of sin simply by observation and reflection; he should not have to learn it by personal experience. Some Christians don't seem to buy this. People say, "How can I really know the evil effects of drink unless I experience them?" The answer is simple. "Go down on skid row and observe what drinking has done to the derelicts. Then reflect on what it will do to you if you follow their example."

A chaplain on board ship became involved in a

If you have a problem too difficult to handle by yourself, seek the Lord's help. He may not solve this problem for you in just the way you had envisioned, but He will solve it.

poker game one night with some younger officers. He won $2,300. When asked about his testimony he laughingly said, "I wanted to teach them by experience the folly of gambling." It didn't seem to occur to him that they could learn by observation and reflection or perhaps even from a sermon he might preach about it. From the chaplain's mode of instruction, they could just as well have learned that gambling is profitable.

As Christians we are to learn by observation and reflection. One of the things to learn by this method is that the believer who cultivates the friendship of the world to the point that he is motivated by wordly plea-sures and worldly desires actually becomes an enemy of God. Everyone needs to check up on himself in this regard. The things of the world are exceedingly attrac-tive in their appeal to fleshly desires. The church of the living God is today greatly handicapped and unable to function at maximum efficiency because of the lack of dedicated personnel.

Jesus in the Sermon on the Mount declared, "No one can serve two masters; for either he will hate the one and love the other, or he will hold to one and despise the other. You cannot serve God and Mammon" (Matt. 6:24). Long ago Joshua challenged the Israelites as the Lord challenges each one today. This great military leader declared, "Choose for yourselves today whom you will serve" (Josh. 24:15). May the answer be the same as Joshua's: "As for me and my house, we will serve the Lord (Josh. 24:15). The individual who follows this modus operandi is truly God's friend.

VERSES 5, 6

In the next question and answer series, James is actually saying, "Are you not aware that the Scriptures teach that in every one of us, yes even in Christians, there is a natural tendency to be envious and jealous of others, to want everything for ourselves, to do that which is displeasing in the sight of the Lord. The natural bent of everyone is toward evil.

"There is a way to overcome it. God is constantly making His grace, which is more than sufficient to meet our needs, available to all. If you have a problem too difficult to handle by yourself, seek the Lord's help. Forget your pride and admit your own limitations. Ask the Lord to help you. He may not solve this problem for you in just the way you had envisioned, but He will solve it. There is no end to His grace which He makes available to you."

A little boy from a family of seven children met with an accident and was taken to the hospital. He came from a rather impoverished home where his hunger was seldom satisfied. If he was served a glass of milk, he had to share it with at least two of his brothers. After the child was made comfortable in the hospital bed, the nurse brought him a large glass of milk. He eyed it carefully and asked timidly, "How deep should I drink?" The nurse assured him he could have it all and there was more from where that came. So it is with God's grace. It is both inexhaustible and constantly available.

FOR REFLECTION

Why are Christians hostile and contentious toward each other?

Can you learn any other way than by experience?

Footnotes

1. *The Letters of James and Peter,* translated and interpreted by William Barclay. Published by the Saint Andrew Press, Edinburgh, 1958; and in the U.S.A. by the Westminster Press, 1961, p. 118.
2. Barclay, *The Letters of James and Peter,* p. 116.
3. Barclay, *The Letters of James and Peter,* p. 116.

CHAPTER TEN

THE PATHWAY TO HONOR

JAMES 4:7-12

JAMES 4:7-12

7. Submit therefore to God. Resist the devil and he will flee from you.
8. Draw near to God and He will draw near to you. Cleanse your hands, you sinners; and purify your hearts, you double-minded.
9. Be miserable and mourn and weep; let your laughter be turned into mourning, and your joy to gloom.
10. Humble yourselves in the presence of the Lord, and He will exalt you.
11. Do not speak against one another, brethren. He who speaks against a brother, or judges his brother, speaks against the law, and judges the law; but if you judge the law, you are not a doer of the law, but a judge *of it.*
12. There is *only* one Lawgiver and Judge, the One who is able to save and to destroy; but who are you who judges your neighbor?

James was concerned about everyone who professed to be a believer. His desire was that each one be a productive Christian—an effective church member. It is an immutable truth that a productive Christian will be an effective church member and an unproductive Christian will not be an effective church member. The two go together like a hand in a glove.

A minister in a rural pastorate was studying the membership rolls and noticed the initials *N.C.* behind a number of names. Puzzled, he asked the church clerk if these letters meant the people had moved to North Carolina. "Of course not," the clerk replied. "N.C. means no 'count."[1]

As the Lord looks at the rolls of today's churches, does He see the letters *N.C.* behind the names of the members?

VERSE 7
Submit

James outlines seven very practical commands for the troublemakers in his church in Jerusalem and through them to all who are potential troublemakers today. The first command is found in the first statement of verse 7. One who submits himself to God is one who places himself under God's control. He makes God the Sovereign of his life. Jesus Christ comes to be not only the Savior but the Lord of his life as well.

One of America's most successful businessmen and greatest financiers was J.L. Kraft, the founder of the Kraft Cheese Company. This busy man was so dedicated to the Lordship of Christ that if he had to be out of town on Wednesday night or if he was sick, he would always wire his pastor to assure him that he would be praying for the midweek service that night. This quality of dedication is a rare jewel in God's sight.

Being under the absolute and complete control of Christ is not a matter of one day under His control and another out from under it. Submitting to the Lord's control is for always. An individual submits himself to Christ for 24 hours a day, 365 days a year whether well or sick, prosperous or impoverished, happy or sad, whether he feels like it or not.

Being under the control of the Lordship of Christ implies that each person will be quick to ascribe all the glory to Him for whatever He may do. It is not a matter of, "Look what I've done for Him." Instead it is, "Look what He has done through me, an insignificant instrument." The glory is always given to Christ.

Anyone who places himself under the control of Christ will be satisfied with whatever station in life he has. He will realize that this is both the place and the circumstances which the Lord has assigned him. Thus he will be free from complaining, grumbling and feeling sorry for himself. He will earnestly seek both to find and to follow the will of God for his life. He will be like the Congolese convert who prayed, "Lord, you be the needle and I will be the thread. You go first and I will follow wherever you lead."

Resist

In the last part of verse 7, Christians are told to resist the devil. James definitely believed and taught that the devil is a person. So many people today are confused about this matter. They seemingly have the impression that when the Bible speaks of the devil, it is referring to an evil influence, an inordinate desire or perhaps that natural tendency toward evil. Nothing is further from the truth than this. The devil is a person. The Bible ascribes to him all of the attributes of personality.

This command carries with it a tremendous promise. The command is to resist the devil. In other words, "Use the willpower God has given you to fight against this ruler of the powers of darkness who is dedicated to your destruction." The promise is that this resistance will result in the devil's fleeing from you.

The word *devil* is a derivative from the Greek verb *diabaloo* which means "to malign, slander, accuse." One of the primary activities in which Satan engages is that of maligning, slandering and accusing God to man. This he does through loaded questions, questions which have inherent within them innuendoes. The purpose of this is to depress man to the extent that he will renounce his faith and live his life either as an agnostic or an atheist. The Christian who allows himself to be depressed and frustrated by the circumstances that come into his life is easily defeated by the adversary. He soon comes to the place where he is of no value to himself, his friends or any worthwhile cause.

If Christians are going to be successful in implementing this command to resist the devil, they need a well-thought-out, definitely planned counterattack to put into operation the moment the devil makes a run. Many times Christians lose the battle before it really begins simply because they have made no previous preparation.

There is a 100 percent foolproof way of defeating the devil and putting him to flight. That way is by a proper use of the Sword of the Spirit which is the Word of God. So important is this way that the Lord Jesus Christ demonstrated it and had that demonstration recorded in Matthew 4:1-11. Here the Savior is attacked three times by the devil. Each time the Master's counterattack was a completely effective, proper use of the Scriptures.

Satan can defeat a person's arguments. He can torpedo his logic and undermine his well-reasoned philosophies. But there is one thing that he cannot do. He cannot overcome the Word of God. The Christian who knows how to use this weapon effectively can put the devil to flight every time.

*T*he greatest biblical revelation is that man, limited as he is, incapable as he is, undeserving as he is, can have a close relationship with the heavenly Father.

A young man doing door-to-door evangelism in Glasgow, Scotland, politely knocked on the door that had just been slammed in his face. Rochunga Pudaite again asked to speak to the occupants for just a minute. "Well, you certainly are persistent," the man said. "My wife is watching television now; we can't be disturbed." But he was weakening. "Only for a minute," Rochunga repeated. The man agreed and the one minute became 10 and then 20 and then 25. Rochunga used Scripture both to show him his need of a Savior and the availability of the Lord Jesus Christ. The next evening both the man and his wife were present at the mass evangelistic meeting and made decisions for Christ.

Rochunga defeated Satan who was trying to keep these people away from Christ. He did it by constantly thrusting the Scriptures forward in the conversation. His own appraisal of the situation was, "You can be a testimony everywhere, if your life is saturated with the Word of God."

VERSE 8
Draw Near to God

The third command, like the first two, is most practical. A good paraphrase of this command is, "Seek close fellowship with the Almighty and as you do, be assured that your efforts will be crowned with success."

It is not enough to resist the devil claiming the promise that by so doing he will flee. This is the negative aspect of the Christian life. The positive aspect is to cultivate a close friendship with the Lord. There are two important realities in this directive: the reality of God's existence and the reality of man's potentially close fellowship with Him.

The first of these realities James accepted by faith. Not once throughout his Epistle does he set forth any argument for God's existence. This truth he held to be self-evident. The person who refuses to accept the fact of God's existence by faith is defeated in life before he gets started. He should be the object of pity and prayer rather than censure.

James knew that God existed, but this is not the whole story. By experience—exciting, confidence-giving, personal experience—he knew that man could have close fellowship with his Creator. This is what gives real meaning and purpose to life. The greatest biblical revelation is that man, limited as he is, incapable as he is, undeserving as he is, can have a close relationship with the heavenly Father.

A little girl attended church by herself one Sunday morning. When she arrived home, her mother asked her about the sermon based on Genesis 5:24. She replied, "Mother, the preacher talked about a man named Enoch. Every day God would visit him at his home and they would take a walk together. One day, instead of turning back when they usually did, they just kept walking. God said, 'Enoch, I have been to your house many times, but you have never been to mine.'" Then the little girl said with great excitement, "Mother, do you know what God did? He took him to His home in heaven!" What a unique picture this is of the God-man relationship available to everyone. No matter where an individual finds himself, God is there and a personal fellowship with Him is available.

The first step in this personal relationship is a personal commitment to Jesus Christ as Savior and Lord. Through this step, man is initiated into the God-man fellowship. Without personal commitment to Christ, man is excluded from this fellowship. The Lord Jesus made this clear when He declared, "I am the way, and the truth, and the life; no one comes to the Father, but through Me" (John 14:6). It is either by Him or we don't get there. It is either by Him or a life without fellowship with the Father.

A great theologian was one day asked, "Isn't conversion the end of the Gospel?" His answer was classic, "Yes, the front end." The initial commitment to Christ as Savior and Lord leads to cultivating a divine fellowship, which begins at the moment of conversion. The more the Christian serves the Lord, the closer he gets to Him and the sweeter his fellowship becomes. Regular church attendance, regular periods of corporate worship with fellow Christians encourage spiritual growth. Devotional reading of the Scriptures cultivates a close fellowship with the Lord. Wise is the Christian who sets time aside every day to read the Scriptures in a devotional manner. The Lord speaks through His Word in a quiet, persuasive manner calling attention to the one truth needed for that moment to strengthen faith and encourage perseverance in Christian witness.

Many Christians complain about not having time for this relationship with the Lord. The businessman who is so occupied in making money that he doesn't take time to eat in a normal way and get his proper rest ends up on his back in the hospital suffering from a heart attack or bleeding ulcers. He is physically bankrupt. So it is with those who do not get proper spiritual nourishment because they don't take time to feed on the Word of God. It isn't long until they are suffering from a spiritual heart attack or a spiritual ulcer.

A practical suggestion for this condition comes out of the experience of a missionary to China. She says, "I found my spiritual life was dragging. I was getting grumpy and down-in-the-mouth and I am afraid my witness for Christ was most unattractive. I decided to remedy the situation by getting up an hour earlier and spending that time in the Word. I confess to you that it has been one of the greatest blessings that has ever come into my life."

Getting up an hour earlier may be hard, but at least 15 minutes earlier allows time for spiritual nourishment and for letting God speak through His Word. This time spent with God and a good recent translation of the Bible will result in one becoming a more effective Christian—a better husband, a better wife, a better student—than ever before.

Close fellowship with the Lord includes daily prayer. God speaks to Christians through the Bible, and they speak to Him in prayer. The two must go together for the Divine-human conversation to be complete. Most Christians believe in the value of daily prayer as a means of enriching their fellowship with the Lord. But it becomes a matter of time—when to pray? A practical answer comes from the pen of Mrs. Louis Evans, Jr., wife of a busy Presbyterian clergyman. At a time when she was raising four young children, she told about her struggle to keep the glow of her Christian testimony. She wrote, "I am now finding little bits of time all through the day when I can talk to God, if I really want to do it." Mrs. Evans continues, "I have learned to pray on the run—on the hoof, as Ruth Graham calls it—in the oddest places and positions; and I have found that God hears those prayers. It doesn't make a bit of difference to him whether I am walking or driving or kneeling or sitting or lying down. God knows the heart and he knows whether we are really praying or not."[2]

Cleanse/Purify

Two phrases stand out in this fourth command. One is "you sinners" and the other is "you double-minded." Four types of church troublemakers are described in verses 2 and 3. Beginning with the fourth verse and continuing on to the end of the chapter, James addresses what he has to say specifically to the troublemakers of his day and through them to troublemakers of every generation. Basic to all the difficulties that arise within the household of faith is the sin of selfishness. Each person has at least a little tinge of this in his makeup. Individuals who allow this sin to become a motivating factor in their lives can't help but cause difficulties among God's people. These are the ones referred to as being sinners and doubleminded.

In the Greek, the word translated as *sinners* means the hardened sinner, the bad man whose sin is open, obvious and notorious, the common criminal. In using it James is saying that the individual who disrupts the harmony of the church because of some selfish desire on his part is in the eyes of God like a common criminal. He is like a thief. When he causes trouble he literally steals from the church her effective testimony in the community where God has placed it to be a witness to the saving grace of the Lord Jesus Christ.

The word *doubleminded* literally means "having two souls." Instead of having one soul that is exclusively the property of Jesus Christ, this person has one that is toward God and another toward the devil. He is spiritually two-faced. His life is one compromise after another.

The command to cleanse and to purify is a demand that Christians let the world know they love Christ by being ethically straight and morally pure. In brief, simple, down-to-earth terms this means that the Christian will be honest in his dealings with his fellowman. The Christian husband will not cheat on his wife and the Christian wife will be faithful to her husband. The Christian young lady will not lower her moral standards simply to be popular or to go along with the crowd. The Christian young man will not make any more demands on his girlfriend than he wants some other boy to make on his sister. The Christian's conversation will be clean, free from obscenity, profanity, smutty jokes and filth.

VERSE 9
Conviction

The fifth and sixth commands are recorded in verses 9 and 10. James very subtly suggests that the reason troublemakers act as they do is that they have never really been converted. They have had no vital, meaningful, personal experience with Jesus Christ. These two verses, 9 and 10, outline what such a person can do in order to correct the situation. The first step is conviction described by the words, *be miserable.* The first step in becoming a Christian is to be convicted of the fact that outside of Christ every individual stands before God as a condemned sinner. This step is absolutely imperative before any person will even be interested in acknowledging Jesus Christ as Savior and Lord.

After being convicted of sin, a man must be truly sorry for that sin of which he is guilty in order to become a Christian. Mourning and weeping are signs of contrition or godly sorrow in the inner man. The words *weep* and *mourn* do not imply that a person must weep actual, physical tears over his sins. Nevertheless, godly sorrow for sins that have been committed is a necessary ingredient in the recipe for eternal redemption.

In order for an individual to become a Christian, he must not only be convicted of his sin and be contrite because of it, he must also be converted. He must change the direction of his life. Instead of going away from the Lord, he must do a right-about-face and begin to walk with the Lord, thinking His thoughts and seeking to conform to His will. The truly repentant person is one whose philosophy of life is changed. The things about which he once laughed are now the things about which he mourns. The things which were once the source of his joy are now the things which cause him great heaviness and depression of soul. Without this third step, conversion or change, there is no repentance.

VERSE 10
Capitulation

Simultaneously with conversion or change, the individual has to take the step of complete surrender to Jesus Christ as Savior and Lord. Conviction, contrition, conversion and capitulation always equal redemption.

One of the South's most sparkling after-dinner speakers and brilliant storytellers used to be the biggest sourpuss south of the Mason-Dixon line. He began to have pains around his heart, pains in his stomach and pains in his joints. He camped on the doorstep of every doctor in town and finally went to a specialist in Chicago who gave him every test known to medical science. After getting the reports of these tests, the specialist explained to him there was nothing wrong with his body but his mind was sick. The specialist said that since the man had come so far for treatment he would give him a prescription. He told him to go home, see his pastor and get some honest-to-God religion. Then he presented a bill of $1,500!

The specialist knew that if the man had to pay enough he would act on his prescription. The man went home calling the specialist a highway robber, but he did go see his pastor. And the pastor knew what to do. He explained to the hypochondriac that what he had to do would cost a lot more than the doctor bill. He said, "You come with me into the church and kneel down and tell the Lord that you are going to give Him everything that you have—your whole self. Tell Him you capitulate completely to Him and that you want Him to be the Savior and Master of your life." This the man did. He poured himself out in a prayer of surrender to the Savior, and the Lord lifted him up and made him a shining example of what Christ can do for a defeated, depressed person.

VERSES 11, 12
Malicious Speech

The seventh and final command deals with the most volatile, the most explosive and the most damaging problem with which the cause of Christ is faced. It is the problem of one church member maliciously gossiping about another. This problem unsolved is like a fire that burns up a building, a cancer that consumes a body, an atomic bomb that levels an entire city or quicksand that buries anything with which it comes in contact.

In dealing with this problem, James does not dilly-dally around. He hits it head on. The word *brethren* is proof positive that this command is aimed directly at Christians for the only brotherhood which the Bible recognizes is the brotherhood in Christ Jesus. The words *speak against* come from a Greek verb usually used in the case of speaking evil of someone else in that person's absence, of criticizing, insulting and slandering someone when he is not there to defend himself.

In effect this command says, "Every time you come upon a small group of people who are maliciously slandering someone not in that group, disassociate yourself immediately from them. Have nothing to do with that activity. Let them know in no uncertain terms that you want no part of their anti-Christian, prodiabolic session. Either speak out against what they are doing or tear yourself away from them so abruptly that they will not miss the point you are attempting to convey."

For some demonic reason most people have a tendency to engage in malicious gossip. The seventeenth century French mystic, Blaise Pascal, put it this way: "I lay it as a fact, that if all men knew what others say of them, there would not be four friends in the world." Once a malicious rumor gets started, it is never possible to undo the damage that it causes.

A young man came to his father asking how he could stop a rumor he had started while angry with a friend. The father told him to distribute a bag of chicken feathers one by one on the doorstep of every home in the neighborhood. After he had done this, the father told him to regather the feathers. The boy tried but the wind had blown many of them away. The father then made the obvious application that the wind of gossip had already taken the rumor far beyond the reach of the young man to stop it.

By using sanctified common sense, which the Bible calls wisdom, much can be done to put a stop to malicious gossiping. One day a faculty member came to a seminary president slandering a fellow professor. The president brought him up short as he said, "Wait just a minute! You can't talk about your colleague in this way unless he is present. I'll call him and have him come to my office. Then you can say whatever you please." The professor's reply was interesting. "Never mind. As I think about it, this is all my fault anyway. Why do I always look for someone else to blame?"

The Christian who speaks evil of another Christian is guilty of two sins. In the first place he is breaking God's law which Jesus summarized in the two great commandments in Matthew 22:37-40. It is impossible for a Christian to love a fellow Christian as he loves himself and at the same time maliciously slander him. If he gossips about him, he doesn't really love him and violates God's law.

Second the slandering, gossiping Christian is guilty of taking over God's prerogative of judgment. When a believer maligns another believer, he is actually guilty of judging that believer. There are many rights and privileges which the Almighty gives to Christians. Just to mention a few, they have the privilege of prayer, the privilege of knowing what is going to take place in the future and the privilege of sharing in the work of the Lord Jesus Christ through His church. There is one privilege which God has reserved for Himself and that is the privilege of judging others.

FOR REFLECTION

What does it mean to you to submit to Jesus Christ?

Who is James talking to when he says, "Do not speak against one another, brethren"? What changes would you see if the Christians in your church obeyed this command?

Footnotes
1. Gaines S. Dobbins, *Great Teachers Make a Difference* (Nashville: Broadman Press), p. 213.
2. Mrs. Louis Evans, DECISION Magazine, © 1962 by The Billy Graham Evangelistic Association.

CHAPTER ELEVEN

CONTINUING ON COURSE

JAMES 4:13—5:6

4:13. Come now, you who say, "Today or tomorrow, we shall go to such and such a city, and spend a year there and engage in business and make a profit."

4:14. Yet you do not know what your life will be like tomorrow. You are *just* a vapor that appears for a little while and then vanishes away.

4:15. Instead, *you ought* to say, "If the Lord wills, we shall live and also do this or that."

4:16. But as it is, you boast in your arrogance; all such boasting is evil.

4:17. Therefore, to one who knows *the* right thing to do, and does not do it, to him it is sin.

5:1. Come now, you rich, weep and howl for your miseries which are coming upon you.

5:2. Your riches have rotted and your garments have become moth-eaten.

5:3. Your gold and your silver have rusted; and their rust will be a witness against you and will consume your flesh like fire. It is in the Last Days that you have stored up your treasure!

5:4. Behold, the pay of the laborers who mowed your field, *and* which has been withheld by you, cries out *against you;* and the outcry of those who did the harvesting has reached the ears of the Lord of Sabaoth.

5:5. You have lived luxuriously on the earth and led a life of wanton pleasure; you have fat-

tened your hearts in a day of slaughter.
5:6. You have condemned and put to death the righteous *man*; he does not resist you.

The Jews in the time James is writing were great merchants and traders. Their world presented them with numerous golden opportunities to exploit their special talents. They lived during the time that new cities were being founded in Europe and in North Africa. The founders of these cities were anxious for the Jews to become citizens of their newly established metropolitan centers. When the Jews came prosperity inevitably followed. Many inducements were given to the people of Israel to leave their native land and take up residence in these new areas.

CHAPTER 4
VERSE 13

The picture in this passage is of one of these Jewish merchants who has received an enticing offer to come to a certain city. As he looks at the map indicating its location, he rubs his hands together greedily and says to himself, "Man, here is a chance for me to make a financial killing. I am going to be in on the ground floor of this juicy deal. I'll get in and get out fast. One year at the most is all that I will need. I'll make a fortune and then life for me will be just one great big bowl of cherries. I'm really going to live it up!"

This merchant made the sad mistake of buying a false philosophy of life. The verb *say* in verse 13 is a translation from the Greek word *legontes* which means "to speak or to say as the result of sound reasoning and careful planning." This man sat down and carefully planned his life on the basis of his own reasoning without taking God into consideration at all. Then he announced what he was going to do.

Practical Atheist

He was behaving as a practical atheist. He didn't stamp his feet, shake his fist toward heaven and cry out that God does not exist. He simply ignored Him. The man made his plans as if he had no responsibility as far as the Almighty is concerned. He went on his merry way alone, thoroughly convinced that he could solve his own problems. Money was his goal and he was not going to let anything stop him from getting it. Not only did this merchant plan his own life, but he bragged about his ability to do so.

Planning without God will lead to frustration, misery, bitterness and ultimate defeat. The greatest military genius that ever lived, Napoleon Bonaparte, learned this lesson the hard way. When he was about to invade Russia, a friend tried to dissuade him. When it became apparent he could not change Napoleon's mind, the friend quoted the familiar proverb, "Man proposes, God disposes." Napoleon, with fires of resentment burning in his heart and flashing in his eyes snapped back, "I dispose as well as propose." A Christian upon hearing this remark said, "I sat that down as the turning point of Bonaparte's fortunes. God will not suffer a creature with impunity to usurp His prerogative." It happened just as this Christian prophesied. Napoleon's invasion of Russia was the beginning of his fall.[1]

There are Christians today who with their hearts really love Jesus Christ. But when it comes to planning

Careful planning of man's life and activities is important providing the Lord is allowed to get in on the ground floor.

their lives, they are practical atheists. They go at it like this—they sit down and decide what they are going to do, then they implement their plans and as an afterthought they pray, "Now, God, I have made this decision. I am hard at work carrying it out. You bless me in it." When He doesn't do so, they become despondent and blame God for letting them down. It never seems to occur to them that perhaps the reason for their failure is that they are out of God's will, that what they want to do is not according to His plan for them.

Beecher once said that if the architect of a house had one plan and the contractor had another, what great conflicts would there be. God is the architect of man's life and man is the contractor. God has a plan. If man has another plan, is it strange that there are clashings and collisions? How much better it is if the contractor follows the architect. How wonderful for man to accept God's will for his life.

Careful planning of man's life and activities is important providing the Lord is allowed to get in on the ground floor. The wise and productive Christian is the one who first of all seeks the mind of God as to what he should do. Then he gets to work implementing God's will in his daily life. Such an individual is assured of God's blessing.

There is one more thing to say about the false philosophy of practical atheism. Many homes today are either shattered or are on the road to being shattered because the husband and wife are practical atheists. They know that it was God who gave the first bride away and performed the first wedding ceremony. It was God who established the home as the basic institution in society. In spite of the fact that they know all of this, they operate their homes as if the Almighty never existed. This is not to say that the Christ-centered home is going to be completely free from trouble. But when trouble does come, God always gives to that Christ-centered home both the grace and the spiritual power to overcome it.

VERSE 14
Life—a Vapor

After pointing out the false philosophy of the materialist, James calls attention to a firm reality, namely that physical life at best is a temporary proposition. This he does with a question and an answer. *Phillips* translates this question and answer, "What, after all, is your life? It is like a puff of smoke visible for a little while and then dissolving into thin air." The *New English Version* of the Bible says, "Your life, what is it? You are no more than a mist, seen for a little while and then dispersing." *The Living Bible* states, "How do you know what is going to happen tomorrow? For the length of your lives is as uncertain as the morning fog—now you see it; soon it is gone."

It is said that long ago when an eastern emperor was crowned at Constantinople, the royal mason would set before his majesty a certain number of marble slabs. One he was to choose then and there for his tombstone. The ancients thought it wise for him to remember his funeral at the time of his coronation as a reminder that his life would not last forever.

The materialist seems to forget that physical life is a fleeting proposition. As he seeks after the things of this world, he gives the impression he believes he is going to live forever. The word translated *appears* in verse 14 is especially descriptive of this person. It comes from the Greek word *phenomenee* and actually means "to show forth, to shine." The rich man in our day does shine. Everybody looks up to him. This possession of wealth and this popularity are only temporary, however, for when the end of his life is approaching, all of his money and all of his popularity will be of little value to him.

The famous Greek philosopher Anaxagoras was once asked why he thought he was born. His answer was a classic, "That I may meditate upon heaven."[2] This is exactly the point—that physical life is temporary. The days here on earth are but a probationary period during which God gives the opportunity to prepare for that which lies ahead in eternity. One time in the Bible the question is asked directly, "What must I do to be saved?" (Acts 16:3 0). The answer is so simply stated that even a child can comprehend it. "Believe in the Lord Jesus Christ and you shall be saved" (Acts 16:31).

VERSES 15, 16, 17

The individual who refuses to prepare in this way, who goes along in his own materialistic way buying the false philosophy of practical atheism, will experience a fatal eventuality. The individual who refuses to do anything to prepare for eternity is guilty of sin. The word *sin* means "to miss the mark." This person is guilty of missing the mark of eternal fellowship with the Almighty. He will spend eternity in hell, separated from God and from his dear ones who made the proper preparation.

The great tragedy is that many contemporary people are so busy going after the almighty dollar and living it up with what they get that they don't have time to even think about God much less prepare for eternity. One of these days the fatal eventuality will come crashing down upon them and there will be no escape. It will be too late.

Someone has said there are four types of people in the world: There are those who are limited as far as their financial holdings are concerned but are extremely wealthy in their relationship to God, there are those who are wealthy both in terms of their finances and their abiding fellowship with the Savior; there are those who are poverty-stricken both in this world and in the world to come; finally some have vast financial holdings today but are completely bankrupt as far as the eternal tomorrow is concerned. These last individuals have a peculiar spelling for the word *God.* They actually spell it *m-o-n-e-y*. It is to this fourth group that James 5:1-6 is addressed.

There are four important lessons to discover in this first part of the fifth chapter. Each has to do with the role that money plays in the life of an individual.

Temporary Wealth

In the first place, material wealth is only a temporary proposition. The man who has it today cannot be guaranteed that he will have it tomorrow. The fact of the matter is, the man who has it in the morning has no guarantee that it will be his that afternoon.

CHAPTER 5
VERSES 1, 2

In ancient times the people in the Near East recognized three types of wealth: the produce of the ground such as grain and corn, wearing apparel, and gold and silver. When a man has a barn full of grain and corn, it is not going to do him any good on a permanent basis for the day will come when that produce will rot. An individual who has his closet completely filled with the most expensive wearing apparel purchased at the most exclusive shops really doesn't have anything of permanent value. Eventually the moths will destroy the clothing. In our day even if the moths don't devour them, in a year's time they will be out of style and of little value.

VERSE 3

To sit back and smugly say, "Silver and gold do not rust, therefore the Bible is not true," is to miss the entire point James is making. He is emphasizing the fact that the very thing the individual does not expect to happen to his money will happen. In one way or another, it will be taken from him. It is not his to keep permanently. And when all that remains from his wealth is rust or that which is of no value, this will be a reminder to him that he has been a fool in making money his god.

The last part of verse 3 sarcastically drives home the point that to be materially wealthy is only a temporary position. William Barclay's paraphrase brings this out, "It is a fine treasure indeed that any man who concentrates on those things is heaping up for himself at the last. The only treasure that he will possess is a consuming fire which will wipe him out." Barclay observes, "It is James's conviction that to concentrate on material things is not only to concentrate on a decaying and corpse-like delusion; it is to concentrate on self-produced destruction and disaster."[3]

Within a few years after James wrote this passage, the rich people in his day who made money their god, the people to whom he immediately addressed it were

The evil connected with money is not to be found in the possession of it but in the way it is accumulated and in the way it is used.

completely wiped out. In A.D. 70 Titus invaded Jerusalem, conquered it and leveled it. These people were either killed or stripped of everything they had and made slaves of the Roman government. Material wealth is void of permanent value.

In the depression of 1929, men went to bed one night as millionaires and woke up the next morning as paupers. The stock market had crashed. Many who had made money their god took what they considered the only way out—suicide.

VERSE 4
Honest Wealth

The means by which material wealth is gained is important. Don't get the impression that the Bible teaches that possession of money is evil. Some of the great men of the Scriptures were wealthy: Abraham, Isaac, Jonah, Elijah, Joseph of Arimathea and Philemon just to mention a few. The evil connected with money is not to be found in the possession of it but in the way it is accumulated and in the way it is used.

The man who by hard work and basic intelligence makes his money honestly is an individual who at this point is worthy of our respect, not censure. One man used his God-given endowment to get ahead in the financial world. In so doing he did not step on nor abuse other people. Just the opposite is true. He paid his employees more and treated them better than his competitors. One of his employees said, "We love our boss; in fact we almost worship him."

James' quarrel is not with men like this. His vendetta is with those men who by ruthlessness and dishonesty have climbed to the top of the financial ladder. In effect verse 4 says, "You have made your money by stealing the wages from those whom you have employed. You live in luxury by keeping these who have worked for you as paupers." And verse 6 follows up the idea by saying, "Whenever someone has tried to stop you in your unscrupulous drive for money, you have used your influence to set up kangaroo courts which have condemned him to death and he has been powerless to resist you."

In the last part of verse 4 there is a warning to these money-mad men. The implication is that they will not get away with this. The Lord of Hosts will ultimately right this injustice and they will be the losers. There is a practical application of this today. The Almighty will take into account honesty, justice and honor when the books of eternity are balanced and the rewards for Christians are handed out.

VERSE 5, 6
Use of Wealth

The use to which Christians put material wealth is of paramount importance. The problem with the man who makes money his god is that he wants to spend everything on himself. His philosophy of life seems to be, "Eat, drink and be merry; indulge to the fullest and forget God, His work and your accountability to Him."

In verse 5 James is saying, "You have amassed a fortune and have spent everything on yourself with no sense of responsibility either to God or your fellowmen." The twentieth century has problems along this line. In Pat Frank's book, *Alas, Babylon*[4] he imagines Florida under the pall of a fictional atomic attack. All electricity is cut off and gasoline supplies are exhausted. Cadillacs are traded for fat hens and power-boats for a shaker of salt. Material things become worse than useless when life settles down to the basics. In *World Aflame*[5] Billy Graham wrote, "We have 'In God We Trust' on our coins but 'Me First' engraved on our hearts."

The next step along this line of thinking may be particularly painful. Those who refuse to tithe are stealing from God. That stolen money actually becomes an idol and for this God is going to hold each person accountable. No one will escape His judgment. Disobedience brings judgment every single time. How much better it would be for all who name Christ as Savior to honor the Lord with what He has entrusted to them, bringing tithes into the storehouse on the first day of the week. There is real joy to be derived from this.

A man came to his pastor and said, "God has prospered me. Therefore, in addition to my regular giving, I want to make a substantial contribution to the church of $129,000." He asked to have the interest from the money used in the college program until such time as a youth center was built. Then he wanted it all to go for that purpose. His countenance exuded joy all the time he was speaking. In a humble way this man was showing that serving the Lord made him truly happy.

Now someone will say, "But I don't have $129,000." The reply is simple. "You do have an income. Give the Lord the first 10 percent which is rightfully His." The promise He has made to the individual who will do this is found in Malachi 3:10.

Ultimate Result

The man who makes money his god will ultimately suffer indescribable loss. The last part of verse 5 is the picture of chickens or sheep who do nothing but feed themselves, being totally oblivious to the fact that they are only preparing themselves for the day of their slaughter. So will it be with those who worship money in order to indulge themselves to the full. They are only preparing themselves for the day of judgment when they shall be eternally consigned to hell.

Those who are all-out for the dollar are saying by the way they live, "I don't believe in judgment. It is an old wives' fable." A farmer was always bragging about being irreligious. He wrote to a local newspaper and said, "Sir, I have been trying an experiment with a field of mine. I plowed it on Sunday, planted it on Sunday, cultivated it on Sunday and reaped it on Sunday. Now, Mr. Editor, what is the result? I have more bushels to the acre in that field than any of my neighbors have this October." The editor in printing the letter commented, "God does not always settle His accounts in October!" The implication is clear. God does settle! Wise is the individual who realizes this and prepares for it by inviting Jesus Christ to be His Savior and Lord.

An old companion of a newly converted Christian one day laughingly asked him, "Can you tell me where hell is?" After a moment of reflection the neophyte believer responded, "Yes, it is at the end of a Christless life."

FOR REFLECTION

How does a practical atheist behave?

What does James mean when he says that life is a vapor?

How can a person be wealthy and be a Christian at the same time?

What happens to the person who makes money his god?

Footnotes

1. Spiros Zodhiates, *The Patience of Hope* (Grand Rapids: Wm. B. Eerdmans Publishing Co., 1960), p. 28.
2. Zodiates, *The Patience of Hope,* p. 163.
3. *The Letters of James and Peter,* translated and interpreted by William Barclay. Published by the Saint Andrew Press, Edinburgh, 1958; and in the U.S.A. by the Westminster Press, 1961, pp. 136,137.
4. Pat Frank, *Alas, Babylon* (Philadelphia; J.B. Lippincott).
5. Billy Graham, *World Aflame* (New York: Doubleday & Company, Inc., 1965), p. 42.

CHAPTER TWELVE

WALKING TALL

JAMES 5:7-20

JAMES 5:7-20

7. Be patient, therefore, brethren, until the coming of the Lord. Behold, the farmer waits for the precious produce of the soil, being patient about it, until it gets the early and late rains.

8. You too be patient; strengthen your hearts, for the coming of the Lord is at hand.

9. Do not complain, brethren, against one another, that you yourselves may not be judged; behold, the Judge is standing right at the door.

10. As an example, brethren, of suffering and patience, take the prophets who spoke in the name of the Lord.

11. Behold, we count those blessed who endured. You have heard of the endurance of Job and have seen the outcome of the Lord's dealings, that the Lord is full of compassion and *is* merciful.

12. But above all, my brethren, do not swear, either by heaven or by earth or with any other oath; but let your yes be yes, and your no, no; so that you may not fall under judgment.

13. Is anyone among you suffering? Let him pray. Is anyone cheerful? Let him sing praises.

14. Is anyone among you sick? Let him call for the elders of the church, and let them pray over him, anointing him with oil in the name of the Lord;

15. and the prayer offered in faith will restore the one who is sick, and the Lord will raise him up, and if he has committed sins, they will be forgiven him.
16. Therefore, confess your sins to one another, and pray for one another, so that you may be healed. The effective prayer of a righteous man can accomplish much.
17. Elijah was a man with a nature like ours, and he prayed earnestly that it might not rain; and it did not rain on earth for three years and six months.
18. And he prayed again, and the sky poured rain, and the earth produced its fruit.
19. My brethren, if any among you strays from the truth, and one turns him back,
20. let him know that he who turns a sinner from the error of his way will save his soul from death, and will cover a multitude of sins.

This important Epistle presents the most practical approach to everyday Christian living to be found in the entire New Testament. Every doctrine is examined in the light of how it affects the believer in his daily walk. This last section points out the practical preparation every Christian should make as he looks forward to the second coming of the Lord Jesus Christ.

Far too many people who claim to love the Lord have a limited idea as to what is involved in adequate preparation for the Savior's second coming. If the average Christian today were asked the question, "What preparation should a person make for the Lord's return?" his answer would be something like this: "In order for an individual to be completely ready for the Second Coming, he must in simple childlike faith accept Jesus Christ as Savior and Lord; once he has done this, he has made all the preparation necessary for this climactic event."

Such an answer is only partially correct. While it is true that the first and most important step in the adequate preparation of the Lord's return is the acceptance of Him in faith as a personal Savior, while it is true that no person without taking this step can possibly be prepared for that event, this answer is by no means complete. The heavenly Father demands far more than this from believers. Once a person has become a Christian, God expects him to put into practice daily the commands that are found in James 5:7-20. Two of these are worded in the negative and five in the positive.

VERSE 7
Be Patient

Positive command number one is stated in the first part of this verse and repeated in verse 8. Notice the word *therefore* in this verse. It actually joins this command with that which precedes it in the Epistle. A careful perusal of this material reveals that the lot of the Christian in this life is not an easy one. Just because of his faith, people will try to take advantage of him and do their best to make his life miserable. He is constantly going to be confronted with problems and difficulties. He is not to worry about this, however, because the day is going to come when the Lord shall return and righteousness shall be enthroned. As he looks forward to

Christians need to prepare for the coming of the Lord by grounding themselves firmly in the Word of God.

that day, the Christian is not to be anxious or disgruntled because of its delay. He is to be patient, being confident in his heart that God is going to keep His promise.

The word translated *patient* comes from the Greek word *makrothumasata* which literally means in this context "to wait with patient expectation." The Christian, knowing that he is never going to be free of harassment in this life, that he is never going to be without problems that are seemingly insolvable, must not allow himself to be frustrated by these things. He is to look forward with patient expectation to that day when the Lord shall return and turn this upside down world right side up.

Here is just a note of caution. The word *patient* does not imply sitting around, doing nothing, waiting for the Savior to come. Christians are to be busy as the farmer is in the last part of verse 7. Those who know anything about farm life are aware that while the husbandman waits for the early and late rain, he is not inactive. He is busy cultivating his fields, spraying the budding crops, making sure his harvesting equipment is in good repair and preparing his barns for the harvest.

VERSE 8
Strengthen Your Hearts

The second positive and practical command is to "strengthen your hearts," to remain firm in the faith. Paul expressed the reason for this, "For there is going to come a time when people won't listen to the truth, but will go around looking for teachers who will tell them just what they want to hear. They won't listen to what the Bible says but will blithely follow their own misguided ideas" (2 Tim. 4:3,4, *TLB*).

That time has come. Christians need to be aware of it to the point that they will prepare for the coming of the Lord by grounding themselves firmly in the Word of God. People for the most part no longer want the truth. They are looking for false teachers who will tell them what they want to hear. And they don't have to look far to find them. They are all around us not only in the cults and the isms, but also in the major Protestant denominations.

Probably the most obnoxious biblical doctrine to the majority of people today is that of the lost condition of a person outside of Christ. They resent being told that because of their refusal to accept Jesus Christ as Savior and Lord they are lost and going to hell. They, therefore, look for teachers and preachers who advocate universal redemption, and they find them.

Those who know the Word of God and are prepared for the Lord's return, know that there is no doctrine of universalism in the Scriptures. The Bible teaches that men outside of Christ are lost. God, through the death, the burial, the resurrection and the second coming of Christ, has provided for man's complete redemption. Man must accept it in faith as a gift from the Almighty. When man receives this gift, the beautiful symphony of salvation becomes a reality in his life.

A Christian worker in Egypt was trying to show a young soldier the way of salvation. The lad was confused for he felt that by his good works he must earn his way into heaven. The Christian kept coming back again and again to the idea that salvation was a gift and that god was offering it to him. Finally the light dawned as the soldier exclaimed, "I see it now! God doesn't expect me to live His life without first giving me His nature."

VERSE 9
Do Not Complain

The first negative command is found in this verse. The word *complain* is most interesting. It comes from the Greek word *stenazo* meaning "to groan, to mutter, to murmur." It has the idea of complaining and criticizing in a negative way. During the Exodus when the children of Israel didn't have as much to eat as they wanted and didn't have the type of food they desired, the Scriptures say in Exodus 16:2 that the whole congregation murmured against Moses and Aaron. They blamed their leaders for their trouble and negatively criticized them because of it.

The *New English Bible* translates verse 9, "Do not blame your troubles on one another." *The Living Bible* puts it this way, "Don't grumble about each other, brothers." The believer is to refrain from complaining against and criticizing his fellow Christians as he looks forward to and prepares for the coming of the Lord.

The last part of verse 9 in effect says, "You Christians who have a tendency to complain and grumble about others and to criticize your fellow church members, need to realize that Almighty God as the Judge of all men stands constantly before the door of each individual's heart. He alone has the prerogative of judgment."

The Christian is to refrain from grumbling about and criticizing his fellow Christians because this always results in his being condemned. He is the loser for doing it. The person indulging in it does irreparable damage to his own personality to the point that he gets to the place where he cannot stand himself. When he is forced to be by himself, he finds the company most annoying and even intolerable at times. The Christian who is guilty of criticizing other Christians makes himself so obnoxious to other people that they don't want to be around him. They avoid him like the plague, so much so that loneliness becomes his greatest problem.

The critical Christian does irreparable damage to the cause of Christ. Non-Christians in looking at him as an example of Christianity are repulsed. They want no part of it. They are driven away from the Savior.

There are three suggestions for the person who has a tendency in this direction: Practice the art of praying for those whom you are tempted to criticize; Practice the art of saying nothing if there is nothing good to say; Realize all Christians are brothers and that each one is to do all that is within his power to overlook the weaknesses of others. This he does by surrounding them with love.

An artist wanted to paint a realistic picture of Alexander the Great. He recognized the fact that in one of his battles, Alexander had received an ugly scar on the side of his face The artist wanted to paint a great likeness of the monarch and at the same time wished to hide the scar. It was not an easy task to accomplish. Finally he painted the great military leader in a reflective attitude with his hand placed against his head and his finger covering the scar.

Christians are not without their faults and their scars. No one in this life is perfect. Therefore, each person would do well not to dwell upon the faults of his fellow Christians. When speaking of another believer, adopt the painter's plan and let the finger of love be placed over the scar thereby concealing it from the unbeliever. God grant that the devil shall not have a field day at the expense of some Christians indulging themselves in the overt criticism of others who love the Lord.

VERSES 10, 11

PERSEVERE

Verses 10 and 11 are illustrations of those who are strong-hearted and do not complain. These men, though they were abused, thrown into prison, beaten, spit upon and maligned in every way patiently endured these hardships as they continued to thunder forth the message of righteousness, which God had given them to proclaim.

All the time Job was undergoing the hardships through which Satan under God's permissive will put him, he patiently and with deep conviction contended for his faith in the Almighty. In the end God dealt with him on the basis of pity, mercy and compassion. Just as the prophets in the midst of great difficulty continued to serve God, and just as Job, while experiencing excruciating suffering and pain, contended for his faith in the Almighty, so Christians who love the Lord Jesus while patiently waiting for His return are to serve Him. This they are to do by making themselves available to the Holy Spirit as instruments in His hand to build the Church and carry out the Great Commission. They are to have the same philosophy as the preacher who is nearly 80 and has been serving in one pastorate for almost 50 years. Asked when he was going to retire, he said, "Never. I would rather die out than rust out!" Many Christians today because of their unwillingness to be active for the Savior are literally rusting out and are therefore worthless in His cause.

VERSE 12
Do Not Swear

The second negative command in James 5:12 is similar

to a command found in the Sermon on the Mount in Matthew 5:34-37. In both of these commands the Scriptures are saying that a Christian should be so honest that his word need not be backed up by an oath. Beyond any doubt, the Christian's word should be as good as his bond. The Scriptures teach absolute honesty both with man and with God. The coin of honesty has two sides.

Christians are to be absolutely honest in dealings with other people. The purpose of this should be obvious. The Christian who is honest will draw people to his Savior. The one who is not will drive them away. Christians are to be absolutely honest with God. Legion are the nominal Christians who would not think of being dishonest with their fellowmen but do not hesitate to be blatantly and defiantly dishonest with God. These people come to church on Sunday morning when it is convenient and sing with great gusto, "I'll say what you want me to say, dear Lord; I'll be what you want me to be."[1] They don't mean this at all. They would never consider tithing; they wouldn't think of being faithful on Sunday night and Wednesday night. It would never occur to them to talk to a lost person about his need of Christ. These people are dishonest with God and at this point are not ready for the Lord's return.

VERSE 13
Pray

This is an easy command to state but an exceedingly difficult one to put into practice. It is especially true today because of the tight schedules that most people keep. Time is at a premium. Most people believe in prayer, yes, but they don't have enough hours in the day to practice it unless suddenly confronted with some grave crisis. Then it is amazing how much time they can find for this purpose.

A careful analysis of verses 13-18 reveals that God expects the Christian to be prayerful in time of affliction, in time of happiness and in time of sickness. In so doing he is assured that the Almighty will hear and answer his prayers according to His will.

During the public ministry of our Lord, one of the great emphases of His preaching was that His followers were not to be frustrated when confronted with difficulties and trouble. They were to make them a matter of prayer. His most famous message dealing with this down-to-earth consideration is recorded in Luke 18:1-8. Jesus introduced His sermon by pointing out that when a person is faced with trouble there are two ways to go. First he can try to handle it himself and ultimately be overcome by it to the point of becoming faint and frustrated. Or he can go the second way, that of presenting his trouble to the heavenly Father in prayer. He implies that this second alternative is the one to follow.

The point that most people miss in this message when it comes to facing trouble is that of being importunate, that of persevering in prayer and that of keeping on until the answer comes. There are people who when confronted with difficulties and problems will pray briefly about them. Then if nothing happens, they will quit, figuring that God just doesn't hear and answer their prayers. Some even get mad. The problem here is not with God, it is with the individual who doesn't carry out His instructions.

The Christian preparing for the Lord's return is to be prayerful in times of great happiness and joy. Examine the last part of verse 13. Oftentimes when things are going their way and all seems to be sweetness and light, people forget about the Lord. It just doesn't seem to occur to them that what they call good fortune is not the result of what they deserve but of His mercy and blessings. At such a time they should be praising the Lord.

VERSES 14, 15
Pray in Sickness

The Christian preparing for the second coming of the Savior is to be prayerful in times of physical sickness. Scripture here is positive in its approach that anointing and praying for the sick is a biblical pattern. It does not mean to imply that physicians do not have their place in society. The physician Luke, for example, was given the privilege of writing two of the New Testament books— the Gospel which bears his name and the book of Acts. He also traveled with Paul on many of his missionary journeys and took care of the distinguished apostle.

The noted physician Ambrose Pere had it right when he displayed a sign in his office which said, "Dr. Pere treats wounds, God heals them." The Christians were instructed to anoint with oil and pray—medicine and prayer. Both are a part of the healing process.

VERSES 16, 17, 18
Confess

The fourth positive command is recorded in the first part of verse 16. A good two-word summary would be, "make restitution." The verb in this command is in the historical present tense, indicating continuous action or a never-ending process. Everytime a Christian does something that offends a fellow Christian he is to go to that brother or sister in Christ, confess his wrongdoing and ask for his or her forgiveness.

This is one of those commands that is easy to say but difficult to practice. There is a large and ominous stumbling block in the way which precludes obedience. This stumbling block, this invisible mountain is called pride. Carrying out the command to confess faults means a person must swallow his pride by admitting his wrongdoing to the person he has harmed and then cast himself upon his mercy, seeking to get back into his good graces. This is hard. Most people would rather take a beating than do it. And yet, this is God's will and it pays great dividends in the work of Christ here and now.

A church was having great difficulty because of two feuding deacons. The young minister was preaching the gospel in a forthright and intelligent manner. The Sunday School was staffed by dedicated and capable teachers and the program of the church was geared to meet the needs of all the people. But the blessings of the Holy Spirit were being witheld from that church. One day one of the deacons awakened to the reason for the situation. He did as every Christian in similar circum-stances should do. He humbled himself by calling the deacon with whom he was feuding and asked him and his wife to come to dinner.

The first deacon's wife prepared a lovely dinner served in a candlelight setting. After dinner the host took his guest into his den where a fire burned brightly in the fireplace. They sat there talking and then the host said, "I have wronged you. I have thought unchristian thoughts concerning you and said harmful things about you that have no basis in fact. I have asked God to forgive me and now I seek your forgiveness. I have no excuse. I have simply done wrong. As a result our church is not what it should be. Will you accept my apology so that once again you and I may walk together as Christian brothers?"

An immediate affirmative answer was given. And a revival began that night in the den of that deacon's home which spread throughout the church.

James goes on from confession of faults to point out that God always answers prayer. Elijah prayed first to withhold the rain and then to send it—just so, God answers the prayers of Christian people.

There is one more point that needs to be made. The book of James does not stand alone. It is part of the whole corpus of the Scriptures. Other sections of the word teach that God's answer to prayer is based on His will in every situation. He always answers, but sometimes the answer is no.

VERSES 19, 20
Witnessing

The final command is revealed in these verses. James simply emphasizes the main business in which the Christian is to be engaged as he waits for and looks for the Lord's second coming. The Master Himself gives this command in a little different manner in Acts 1:8. Shortly before the ascension, the disciples came to the Savior and in effect asked Him to pinpoint the time of the establishing of His earthly reign. This was just another way of inquiring about the time element in His second coming. Jesus gave them a straightforward answer. Almighty God expects Christians to be witnessing as they prepare for the Lord's return.

It is the Christians' great responsibility and their high privilege to let all people know both at home and abroad that the regenerating power of the Omnipotent God of the universe is available through the Lord Jesus Christ. He has provided for them what they cannot provide for themselves—eternal redemption. Redemption when accepted by faith will result in their lives being transformed and all things becoming new in the sense of being God-centered. Anyone, regardless of race or economic standing, by calling in faith upon Jesus Christ can have as a personal gift from God this redemption. Only as men experience this God-given transformation in their lives is there a chance for society to be changed for the better.

FOR REFLECTION

List the demands God makes of the Christian in James 5:7-20.

Why is confession to one another an important part of your life as a Christian?

Footnote
1. "I'll Go Where You Want Me to Go," *Great Hymns of the Faith* (Grand Rapids: Zondervan Publishing House, 1968), p. 440.